Respectfully
Fanny Kelly

MY CAPTIVITY
Among the
SIOUX INDIANS

by Fanny Kelly

APPLEWOOD BOOKS
Bedford, Massachusetts

My Captivity Among the Sioux Indians
was originally published in 1871.

Thank you for purchasing an Applewood book.
Applewood reprints America's lively classics—
books from the past that are still of interest to
modern readers. For a free copy of our current
catalog, write to:

Applewood Books
P.O. Box 365
Bedford, MA 01730

ISBN: 0-918222-97-4

NARRATIVE

OF

MY CAPTIVITY

AMONG THE

SIOUX INDIANS.

BY

FANNY KELLY.

WITH A BRIEF ACCOUNT OF GENERAL SULLY'S INDIAN EXPEDITION IN 1864,
BEARING UPON EVENTS OCCURRING IN MY CAPTIVITY.

HARTFORD, CONN.
MUTUAL PUBLISHING COMPANY.

DEDICATION.

INTRODUCTORY.

THE summer of 1864 marked a period of unusual peril to the daring pioneers seeking homes in the far West. Following upon the horrible massacres in Minnesota in 1862, and the subsequent chastisements inflicted by the expeditions under Generals Sully and Sibley in 1863, whereby the Indians were driven from the then western borders of civilization, in Iowa, Minnesota, and the white settlements of Dakota, in the Missouri Valley, the great emigrant trails to Idaho and Montana became the scene of fresh outrages; and, from the wild, almost inaccessible nature of the country, pursuit and punishment were impossible.

I was a member of a small company of emigrants, who were attacked by an overwhelming force of hostile Sioux, which resulted in the death of a large proportion of the party, in my own capture, and a horrible captivity of five months' duration.

Of my thrilling adventures and experience during this season of terror and privation, I propose to give a plain, unvarnished narrative, hoping the reader will be more interested in facts concerning the habits, manners, and customs of the Indians, and their treatment of prisoners, than in theoretical speculations and fine-wrought sentences.

Some explanation is due the public for the delay in publishing this my narrative. From memoranda, kept during the period of my captivity, I had completed the work for publication, when the manuscript was purloined and published; but the work was suppressed before it could be placed before the public. After surmounting many obstacles, I have at last succeeded in gathering the scattered fragments; and, by the aid of memory, impressed as I pray no mortal's may ever be again, am enabled to place the results before, I trust, a kind-judging, appreciative public.

CONTENTS.

(vii)

CHAPTER XV.

CHAPTER XVI.

CHAPTER XVII.

CHAPTER XVIII.

CHAPTER XIX.

CHAPTER XX.

CHAPTER XXI.

CHAPTER XXII.

CHAPTER XXIII.

CHAPTER XXIV.

CHAPTER XXV.

CHAPTER XXVI.

CHAPTER XXVII.

CHAPTER XXVIII.

CAPTIVITY AMONG THE SIOUX.

CHAPTER I.

EARLY HISTORY—CANADA TO KANSAS—DEATH OF MY FATHER—MY
MARRIAGE—"HO! FOR IDAHO!"—CROSSING THE PLATTE RIVER—
A STORM.

I WAS born in Orillia, Canada, in 1845. Our home
was on the lake shore, and there amid pleasant surroundings I passed the happy days of early childhood.

The years 1852 to 1856 witnessed, probably, the
heavest immigration the West has ever known in a
corresponding length of time. Those who had gone
before sent back to their friends such marvelous ac-
counts of the fertility of the soil, the rapid develop-
ment of the country, and the ease with which fortunes
were made, the "Western fever" became almost epi-
demic. Whole towns in the old, Eastern States were
almost depopulated. Old substantial farmers, surrounded apparently by all the comforts that heart
could wish, sacrificed the homes wherein their families
had been reared for generations, and, with all their
worldly possessions, turned their faces toward the set-

ting sun. And with what high hopes! Alas! how few, comparatively, met their realization.

In 1856, my father, James Wiggins, joined a New York colony bound for Kansas. Being favorably impressed with the country and its people, they located the town of Geneva, and my father returned for his family.

Reaching the Missouri River on our way to our new home, my father was attacked with cholera, and died.

In obedience to his dying instructions, my widowed mother, with her little family, continued on the way to our new home. But, oh! with what saddened hearts we entered into its possession. It seemed as if the light of our life had gone out. He who had been before to prepare that home for us, was not there to share it with us, and, far away from all early associations, almost alone in a new and sparsely settled country, it seemed as though hope had died.

But God is merciful. He prepares the soul for its burdens. Of a truth, "He tempers the wind to the shorn lamb."

Our family remained in this pleasant prairie home, where I was married to Josiah S. Kelly.

My husband's health failing, he resolved upon a change of climate. Accordingly, on the 17th of May, 1864, a party of six persons, consisting of Mr. Gardner Wakefield, my husband, myself, our adopted daughter (my sister's child), and two colored servants, started from Geneva, with high-wrought hopes and pleasant anticipations of a romantic and delightful journey across the plains, and a confident expectation of future prosperity among the golden hills of Idaho.

A few days after commencing our journey, we were joined by Mr. Sharp, a Methodist clergyman, from Verdigris River, about thirty miles south of Geneva; and, a few weeks later, we overtook a large train of emigrants, among whom were a family from Allen County with whom we were acquainted—Mr. Larimer, wife, and child, a boy eight years old. Preferring to travel with our small train, they left the larger one and became members of our party. The addition of one of my own sex to our little company was cause of much rejoicing to me, and helped relieve the dullness of our tiresome march.

The hours of noon and evening rest were spent in preparing our frugal meals, gathering flowers with our children, picking berries, hunting curiosities, or gazing in wrapt wonder and admiration at the beauties of this strange, bewildering country.

Our amusements were varied. Singing, reading, writing to friends at home, or pleasant conversation, occupied our leisure hours.

So passed the first few happy days of our emigration to the land of sunshine and flowers.

When the sun had set, when his last rays were flecking the towering peaks of the Rocky Mountains, gathering around the camp-fires, in our home-like tent, we ate with a relish known only to those who, like us, scented the pure air, and lived as nature demanded.

At night, when our camp had been arranged by Andy and Franklin, our colored men, it was always in the same relative position, Mr. Kelly riding a few miles ahead as evening drew near to select the camping ground.

The atmosphere, which during the day was hot and stifling, became cool, and was laden with the odor of prairie flowers, the night dews filling their beautiful cups with the waters of heaven.

The solemnity of night pervaded every thing. The warblings of the feathered tribe had ceased. The antelope and deer rested on the hills; no sound of laughing, noisy children, as in a settled country; no tramping of busy feet, or hurrying to and fro. All is silent. Nature, like man, has put aside the labors of the day, and is enjoying rest and peace.

Yonder, as a tiny spark, as a distant star, might be seen from the road a little camp-fire in the darkness spread over the earth.

Every eye in our little company is closed, every hand still, as we lay in our snugly-covered wagons, awaiting the dawn of another day.

And the Eye that never sleeps watched over us in our lonely camp, and cared for the slumbering travelers.

Mr. Wakefield, with whom we became acquainted after he came to settle at Geneva, proved a most agreeable companion. Affable and courteous, unselfish, and a gentleman, we remember him with profound respect.

A fine bridge crosses the Kansas River. A half-hour's ride through the dense heavy timber, over a jet-black soil of incalculable richness, brought us to this bridge, which we crossed.

We then beheld the lovely valley of the prairies, intersecting the deep green of graceful slopes, where waves tall prairie grass, among which the wild flowers grow.

Over hundreds of acres these blossoms are scattered, yellow, purple, white, and blue, making the earth look like a rich carpet of variegated colors; those blooming in spring are of tender, modest hue, in later summer and early autumn clothed in gorgeous splendor. Solomon's gold and purple could not outrival them.

Nature seemingly reveled in beauty, for beauty's sake alone, for none but the simple children of the forest to view her in state.

Slowly the myriad years come and go upon her solitary places. Tender spring-time and glorious summer drop down their gifts from overflowing coffers, while the steps of bounding deer or the notes of singing birds break upon the lonely air.

The sky is of wonderful clearness and transparency. Narrow belts and fringes of forest mark the way of winding streams.

In the distance rise conical mounds, wrapped in the soft veil of dim and dreamy haze.

Upon the beaten road are emigrants wending their way, their household goods packed in long covered wagons, drawn by oxen, mules, or horses; speculators working their way to some new town with women and children; and we meet with half-breed girls, with heavy eye-lashes and sun-burnt cheeks, jogging along on horseback.

I was surprised to see so many women among the emigrants, and to see how easily they adapted themselves to the hardships experienced in a journey across the plains.

As a rule, the emigrants travel without tents, sleeping in and under wagons, without removing their clothing.

Cooking among emigrants to the far West is a very primitive operation, a frying-pan and perhaps a Dutch oven comprising the major part of the kitchen furniture.

The scarcity of timber is a source of great inconvenience and discomfort, "buffalo chips" being the substitute. At some of the stations, where opportunity offered, Mr. Kelly bought wood by the pound, as I had not yet been long enough inured to plains privations to relish food cooked over a fire made with "chips" of that kind.

We crossed the Platte River by binding four wagon

boxes together, then loaded the boat with goods, and
were rowed across by about twenty men.

We were several days in crossing. Our cattle and
horses swam across. The air had been heavy and op-
pressively hot; now the sky began to darken suddenly,
and just as we reached the opposite shore, a gleam of
lightning, like a forked tongue of flame, shot out of
the black clouds, blinding us by its flash, and followed
by a frightful crash of thunder.

Another gleam and another crash followed, and the
dense blackness lowered threateningly over us, almost
shutting out the heights beyond, and seeming to en-
circle us like prisoners in the valley that lay at our
feet.

The vivid flashes lighting the darkness for an instant
only made its gloom more fearful, and the heavy rolling of the thunder seemed almost to rend the heavens above it.

All at once it burst upon our unprotected heads in
rain. But such rain! Not the gentle droppings of an
afternoon shower, nor a commonplace storm, but a
sweeping avalanche of water, drenching us completely
at the first dash, and continuing to pour, seeming to
threaten the earth on which we stood, and tempt the
old Platte to rise and claim it as its own.

Our wagon covers had been removed in the fording,
and we had no time to put up tents for our protection
until its fury was exhausted. And so we were forced

to brave the elements, with part of our company on the other side of the swollen river, and a wild scene, we could scarcely discern through the pelting rain, surrounding us.

One soon becomes heroic in an open-air life, and so we put up what shelter we could when the abating storm gave us opportunity; and, wringing the water out of clothes, hair, and eye-brows, we camped in cheerful hope of a bright to-morrow, which did not disappoint us, and our hundreds of emigrant companions scattered on the way.

Each recurring Sabbath was gratefully hailed as a season of thought and repose; as a matter of conscience and duty we observed the day, and took pleasure in doing so.

We had divine service performed, observing the ceremonies of prayer, preaching, and singing, which was fully appreciated in our absence from home and its religious privileges.

Twenty-five miles from California Crossing is a place called Ash Hollow, where the eye is lost in space as it endeavors to penetrate its depths. Here some years before, General Harney made his name famous by an indiscriminate massacre of a band of hostile Indians, with their women and children.

THE CAMP.

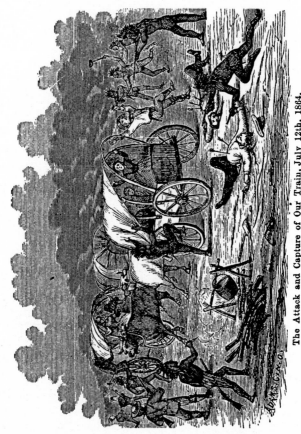

The Attack and Capture of Our Train, July 12th, 1864.

CHAPTER II.

THE ATTACK AND THE CAPTURE.

A TRAIN of wagons were coursing their westward way, with visions of the future bright as our own. Sometimes a single team might be seen traveling alone.

Our party were among the many small squads emigrating to the land of promise.

The day on which our doomed family were scattered and killed was the 12th of July, a warm and oppressive day. The burning sun poured forth its hottest rays upon the great Black Hills and the vast plains of Montana, and the great emigrant road was strewed with men, women, and children, and flocks of cattle, representing towns of adventurers.

We looked anxiously forward to the approach of evening, with a sense of relief, after the excessive heat of the day.

Our journey had been pleasant, but toilsome, for we had been long weeks on the road.

Slowly our wagons wound through the timber that skirted the Little Box Elder, and, crossing the stream, we ascended the opposite bank.

We had no thought of danger or timid misgivings on the subject of savages, for our fears had been all dispersed by constantly received assurances of their friendliness.

At the outposts and ranches, we heard nothing but ridicule of their pretensions to warfare, and at Fort Laramie, where information that should have been reliable was given us, we had renewed assurances of the safety of the road and friendliness of the Indians.

At Horseshoe Creek, which we had just left, and where there was a telegraph station, our inquiries had elicited similar assurances as to the quiet and peaceful state of the country through which we must pass.

Being thus persuaded that fears were groundless, we entertained none, and, as I have mentioned before, our small company preferred to travel alone on account of the greater progress made in that way.

The beauty of the sunset and the scenery around us filled our hearts with joy, and Mr. Wakefield's voice was heard in song for the last time, as he sang, "Ho! for Idaho." Little Mary's low, sweet voice, too, joined in the chorus. She was so happy in her childish glee on that day, as she always was. She was the star and joy of our whole party.

We wended our way peacefully and cheerfully on, without a thought of the danger that was lying like a tiger in ambush in our path.

Without a sound of preparation or a word of warning, the bluffs before us were covered with a party of about two hundred and fifty Indians, painted and equipped for war, who uttered the wild war-whoop and fired a signal volley of guns and revolvers into the air.

This terrible and unexpected apparition came upon us with such startling swiftness that we had not time to think before the main body halted and sent out a part of their force, which circled us round at regular intervals, but some distance from our wagons. Recovering from the shock, our men instantly resolved on defense, and corralled the wagons. My husband was looked upon as leader, as he was principal owner of the train. Without regard to the insignificance of our numbers, Mr. Kelly was ready to stand his ground; but, with all the power I could command, I entreated him to forbear and only attempt conciliation. "If you fire one shot," I said, "I feel sure you will seal our fate, as they seem to outnumber us ten to one, and will at once massacre all of us."

Love for the trembling little girl at my side, my husband, and friends, made me strong to protest against any thing that would lessen our chance for escape with our lives. Poor little Mary! from the first she had entertained an ungovernable dread of the Indians, a repugnance that could not be overcome, although in our intercourse with friendly savages, I had endeavored to show how unfounded it was, and persuade her that they were civil and harmless, but all in vain. Mr.

Kelly bought her beads and many little presents from them which she much admired, but she would always add, "They look so cross at me and they have knives and tomahawks, and I fear they will kill me." Could it be that her tender young mind had some presentiment or warning of her horrid fate?

My husband advanced to meet the chief and demand his intentions.

The savage leader immediately came toward him, riding forward and uttering the words, "How! how!" which are understood to mean a friendly salutation.

His name was Ottawa, and he was a war chief of the Ogalalla band of the Sioux nation. He struck himself on his breast, saying, "Good Indian, me," and pointing to those around him, he continued, "Heap good Indian, hunt buffalo and deer." He assured us of his utmost friendship for the white people; then he shook hands, and his band followed his example, crowding around our wagons, shaking us all by the hand over and over again, until our arms ached, and grinning and nodding with every demonstration of good will.

Our only policy seemed to be temporizing, in hope of assistance approaching; and, to gain time, we allowed them unopposed to do whatever they fancied. First, they said they would like to change one of their horses for the one Mr. Kelly was riding, a favorite race horse. Very much against his will, he acceded to their request, and gave up to them the noble animal to which he was fondly attached.

My husband came to me with words of cheer and hope, but oh! what a marked look of despair was upon his face, such as I had never seen before.

The Indians asked for flour, and we gave them what they wanted of provisions. The flour they emptied upon the ground, saving only the sack. They talked to us partly by signs and partly in broken English, with which some of them were quite familiar, and as we were anxious to suit ourselves to their whims and preserve a friendly intercourse as long as possible, we allowed them to take whatever they desired, and offered them many presents besides. It was, as I have said before, extremely warm weather, but they remarked that the cold made it necessary for them to look for clothing, and begged for some from our stock, which was granted without the slightest offered objection on our part. I, in a careless-like manner, said they must give me some moccasins for some articles of clothing that I had just handed them, and very pleasantly a young Indian gave me a nice pair, richly embroidered with different colored beads.

Our anxiety to conciliate them increased every moment, for the hope of help arriving from some quarter grew stronger as they dallied, and, alas! it was our only one.

They grew bolder and more insolent in their advances. One of them laid hold of my husband's gun, but, being repulsed, desisted.

The chief at last intimated that he desired us to proceed on our way, promising that we should not be molested. We obeyed, without trusting them, and soon the train was again in motion, the Indians insisting on driving our herd, and growing ominously familiar. Soon my husband called a halt. He saw that we were approaching a rocky glen, in whose gloomy depths he anticipated a murderous attack, and from which escape would be utterly impossible. Our enemies urged us still forward, but we resolutely refused to stir, when they requested that we should prepare supper, which they said they would share with us, and then go to the hills to sleep. The men of our party concluded it best to give them a feast. Mr. Kelly gave orders to our two colored servants to prepare at once to make a feast for the Indians.

Andy said, " I think, if I knows any thing about it, they 's had their supper ;" as they had been eating sugar crackers from our wagons for an hour or more.

The two colored men had been slaves among the Cherokees, and knew the Indian character by experience. Their fear and horror of them was unbounded, and their terror seemed pitiable to us, as they had worked for us a long time, and were , most faithful, trustworthy servants.

Each man was busy preparing the supper; Mr.

Larimer and Frank were making the fire; Mr. Wakefield was getting provisions out of the wagon; Mr. Taylor was attending to his team; Mr. Kelly and Andy were out some distance gathering wood; Mr. Sharp was distributing sugar among the Indians; supper, that they asked for, was in rapid progress of preparation, when suddenly our terrible enemies threw off their masks and displayed their truly demoniac natures. There was a simultaneous discharge of arms, and when the cloud of smoke cleared away, I could see the retreating form of Mr. Larimer and the slow motion of poor Mr. Wakefield, for he was mortally wounded.

Mr. Kelly and Andy made a miraculous escape with their lives. Mr. Sharp was killed within a few feet of me. Mr. Taylor—I never can forget his face as I saw him shot through the forehead with a rifle ball. He looked at me as he fell backward to the ground a corpse. I was the last object that met his dying gaze. Our poor faithful Frank fell at my feet pierced by many arrows. I recall the scene with a sickening horror. I could not see my husband anywhere, and did not know his fate, but feared and trembled. With a glance at my surroundings, my senses seemed gone for a time, but I could only live and endure.

I had but little time for thought, for the Indians quickly sprang into our wagons, tearing off covers, breaking, crushing, and smashing all hinderances to plunder, breaking open locks, trunks, and boxes, and distributing or destroying our goods with great rapidity, using their tomahawks to pry open boxes, which they split up in savage recklessness.

Oh, what horrible sights met my view! Pen is powerless to portray the scenes occurring around me. They filled the air with the fearful war-whoops and hideous shouts. I endeavored to keep my fears quiet as possible, knowing that an indiscreet act on my part might result in jeopardizing our lives, though I felt certain that we two helpless women would share death by their hands; but with as much of an air of indifference as I could command, I kept still, hoping to prolong our lives, even if but a few moments. I was not allowed this quiet but a moment, when two of the most savage-looking of the party rushed up into my wagon, with tomahawks drawn in their right hands, and with their left seized me by both hands and pulled me violently to the ground, injuring my limbs very severely, almost breaking them, from the effects of which I afterward suffered a great deal. I turned to my little Mary, who, with outstretched hands, was standing in the wagon, took her in my arms and helped her to the ground. I then turned to the chief, put my hand upon his arm, and implored his protection for my fellow-prisoner and our children. At first he gave me no hope, but seemed utterly indifferent to my prayers. Partly in words and partly by signs, he

ordered me to remain quiet, placing his hand upon his
revolver, that hung in a belt at his side, as an argument to enforce obedience.

A short distance in the rear of our train a wagon
was in sight. The chief immediately dispatched a de-
tachment of his band to capture or to cut it off from us,
and I saw them ride furiously off in pursuit of the
small party, which consisted only of one family and
a man who rode in advance of the single wagon.
The horseman was almost instantly surrounded and
killed by a volley of arrows. The husband of the
family quickly turned his team around and started
them at full speed, gave the whip and lines to his wife,
who held close in her arms her youngest child. He
then went to the back end of his wagon and threw
out boxes, trunks, every thing that he possessed. His
wife meantime gave all her mind and strength to urging the horses forward on their flight from death. The
Indians had by this time come very near, so that they
riddled the wagon-cover with bullets and arrows, one
passing through the sleeve of the child's dress in its
mother's arms, but doing it no personal injury.

The terrified man kept the Indians at bay with his
revolver, and finally they left him and rode furiously
back to the scene of the murder of our train.

CHAPTER III.

MY HUSBAND'S ESCAPE—BURIAL OF THE DEAD—ARRIVAL OF THE
SURVIVORS AT DEER CREEK—AN ILL-TIMED BALL.

WHEN the Indians fired their fatal volley into the
midst of our little company, while yet they were preparing to entertain them with a hospitable supper, my
husband was some distance from the scene of horror;
but, startled by the unexpected report, he hurriedly
glanced around, saw the pale, terror-stricken faces of
his wife and child, and the fall of Rev. Mr. Sharp
from the wagon, while in the act of reaching for sugar
and other articles of food with which to conciliate our
savage guests. The hopelessness of the situation struck
a chill to his heart. Having laid down his gun to
assist in the preparation of the feast, the utter futility
of contending single-handed against such a host of
infuriated demons was too apparent. His only hope,
and that a slight one indeed, was that the Indians
might spare the lives of his wife and child, to obtain
a ransom. In this hope he resolved upon efforts for
the preservation of his own life, that he might after-

ward put forth efforts for our rescue, either by pursuit and strategy, or by purchase.

He was shot at, and the barbed arrows whizzed past him, some passing through his clothing. He saw Mr. Wakefield fall, and knew that he was wounded, if not killed. Mr. Larimer passed him in his flight for life toward some neighboring timber.

Mr. Kelly then ran for some tall grass and sage brush, where he concealed himself, favored by the fast approaching darkness. Scarcely daring to breathe, his mind tortured with agonizing fears for the fate of his wife and child, he seemed to hear from them the cry for help, and at one time resolved to rush to their rescue, or die with them; any fate seemed better than such torturing doubt. But, realizing at last the utter hopelessness of an attempt at rescue, and knowing that it was a custom of the Indians, sometimes, to spare the lives of white women and children taken captive, for ransom, he again resolved, if possible, to save his own life, that he might devote all his energies, and the remnant of fortune the savages had not despoiled him of, to the accomplishment of the rescue of his wife and child.

Lying in his perilous shelter, he saw darkness creep slowly around the hills, closing on the scene of murder and devastation, like a curtain of mercy dropped to shut out a hideous sight. He heard the noise of breaking and crashing boxes, and the voices of the

Indians calling to each other; then came the culmination of his awful suspense. The Indians had again mounted their horses, and, raising the terrible war song, chanted its ominous notes as they took their way across the hills, carrying his yearning thoughts with them. Pen is powerless to portray the agony, to him, of those fearful moments.

Still fearing to move in the darkness, he distinguished footsteps near him, and knew by the stealthy tread that they were those of an Indian. In breathless silence he crouched close to the ground, fearing each instant the descent of the tomahawk and the gleam of the scalping-knife, when, strange to say, a venomous reptile came to his rescue, and his enemy fled before it. A huge rattlesnake, one of the many with which that region is infested, raised its curved neck close beside him, and, thrusting forth its poisonous fangs, gave a warning rattle. The prowling Indian took alarm at the sound; other snakes, roused for the safety of their young in the dens around, repeated it, and the savage, knowing it would be death to venture further, retreated, leaving my husband in safety where he had taken refuge; for, although he must have lain close to the noisome reptile, he received no hurt, and the greater horror of his human foe rendered him almost indifferent to the dangers of his surroundings.

Cautiously he crawled out of the weeds and grass,

and, rising to his feet unharmed, started swiftly in an eastward direction. He had to go far out in the hills to avoid the savages, and, after traveling many miles around, he at last reached the large train, with which the small party I had seen pursued had previously taken refuge.

They were already consolidating with other trains for defense, and would not venture to join Mr. Kelly, although he earnestly implored assistance to go out in aid of his friends and family, if any of them should be left alive.

The colored man, Andy, soon after joined them. He came in running and in great excitement, and was about to report all the company killed, when he joyfully discovered Mr. Kelly.

Great consternation and alarm had spread with the tidings of the massacre, and fears for personal safety prevented any one from joining my unhappy husband in efforts to rescue his wife and child, or succor his missing companions.

The train did not move forward until re-enforced by many others along the road; and even then every precaution was taken to secure safety and prevent a surprise. Women in many instances drove the teams, to prevent their husbands or fathers being taken at a disadvantage; weapons were in every man's hands, and vigilant eyes were fixed on every bluff or gorge, anticipating attack.

A little time and travel brought them to the first scene of murder, where they found the dead body of the companion of the man who so narrowly escaped with his family. They placed the body in a wagon, and proceeded to the dreaded spot where the slaughter of our party had occurred.

The wagons still were standing, and feathers, flour, the remnants of much that was but half destroyed, lay scattered about the ground.

Mr. Kelly, with faltering steps, supported by the strong arm of Andy, was among the first to search the spot; his intense distress for the unknown fate of his family urged him on, although he dreaded to think of what the bloody spot might disclose to him.

The dead bodies of Mr. Sharp, Mr. Taylor, and our colored servant, Franklin, were discovered lying where they had fallen. Poor Frank had been shot by an arrow that pierced both his legs, pinning them together, in which condition he had been murdered by the ruthless wretches by having his skull broken.

Both Mr. Sharp and Mr. Taylor left large families at home to mourn their loss. Mr. Larimer came up with an arrow wound in one of his limbs. He had passed the night in trying to elude his savage pursuers, and was very tired and exhausted, and very much distressed about his wife and son, a robust little fellow of eight or nine years.

But Mr. Wakefield was nowhere to be seen. After

searching the brushwood for some time, and a quarter of a mile distant from the scene of attack, they discovered him still alive, but pierced by three arrows that he had vainly endeavored to extract, succeeding only in withdrawing the shafts, but leaving the steel points still deeply imbedded in the flesh. Mr. Kelly took him and cared for him with all the skill and kindness possible. No brothers could have been more tenderly attached to each other than they. He then procured as comfortable a conveyance as he could for them, and picked up a few relics from our demolished train. Among them was a daily journal of our trip, from the time we were married until the hour that the Indians came upon us. This he prized, as he said, more than he did his life.

The next thing that was necessary to do, after the wounded were cared for, was to bury the dead, and a wide grave was dug and the four bodies solemnly consigned, uncoffined, to the earth. A buffalo robe was placed above them, and then the earth was piled on their unconscious breasts.

At that time the question of color had occasioned much dissension, and controversy ran high as to the propriety of allowing the colored people the privilege of sitting beside their white brethren. Poor Franklin had shared death with our companions, and was not deemed unworthy to share the common grave of his fellow victims. They lie together in the valley of

Little Box Elder, where with saddened hearts our friends left them, thinking of the high hopes and fearless energy with which they had started on their journey, each feeling secure in the success that awaited them, and never, for a moment, dreaming of the grave in the wilderness that was to close over them and their earthly hopes. They were buried on the desolate plain, a thousand miles away from their loved wives and children, who bemoan their sad, untimely fate.

Mr. Kelly found part of his herd of cattle grazing near by; Mr. Sharp's were still tied to the stake where he had carefully secured them. The Indians had taken our horses, but left the cattle, as they do when they are on the war path, or unless they need meat for present use. They shot some of them, however, and left them to decay upon the plain. Many arrows were scattered upon the ground, their peculiar marks showing that their owners had all belonged to one tribe, though of different bands. They were similar in form and finish; the shafts were round and three feet long, grooved on their sides, that the blood of the victim might not be impeded in its outward flow; each had three strips of feathers attached to its top, about seven inches in length, and, on the other end, a steel point, fastened lightly, so as to be easily detached in the flesh it penetrates. The depth of the wound depends on the distance of the aim, but they sometimes pass quite through the body, though usually their force is exhausted in entering a few inches beyond the point.

The wounded being made as comfortable as circumstances would allow, the train left the spot in the evening, and moved forward to an encampment a mile distant from the sad place, where the journey of our lost companions had ended forever, whose visions of the golden land must be a higher and brighter one than earthly eyes can claim.

Early next day the travelers arrived at Deer Creek Fort, where Mr. Kelly found medical aid for the wounded, and procured a tent to shelter them, and devoted himself to alleviating their sufferings, and, with the assistance of the kind people of the fort, succeeded in arranging them in tolerable comfort.

Captain Rhineheart was commanding officer at Deer Creek, and ordered the property of the deceased to be delivered over to him, which Mr. Kelly did.

The story of the attack and massacre had traveled faster than the sufferers from its barbarity. The garrison had learned it before the train arrived, through some soldiers returning from Fort Laramie, where they had been to receive money from the paymaster, who had heard an account of the attack on the road, and had a passing glimpse of the terrible field of slaughter.

The evening that the large train arrived at the fort, the officers gave a ball, and the emigrant women were invited, from the trains camped in the vicinity, to join in these inappropriately timed festivities.

The mother of the child, who had so narrowly escaped death, having lost her own wardrobe in her efforts to escape the pursuit of the Indians, borrowed a dress from a lady who resided at the fort, and attended the entertainment, dancing and joining in the gayeties, when the burial of their companion and our poor men had just been completed, and the heavy cloud of our calamity had so lately shrouded them in gloom. Such are the effects of isolation from social and civil influence, and contact with danger, and familiarity with terror and death.

People grow reckless, and often lose the gentle sympathies that alleviate suffering, from frequent intercourse with it in its worst forms.

CHAPTER IV.

BEGINNING OF MY CAPTIVITY.

THE facts related in the preceding chapter concerning matters occurring in Mr. Kelly's experience, and adventures after the attack upon our train, were related to me after my restoration to freedom and my husband, by him.

I now return to the narration of my own terrible experiences.

I was led a short distance from the wagon, with Mary, and told to remain quiet, and tried to submit; but oh, what a yearning sprang up in my heart to escape, as I hoped my husband had done! But many watchful eyes were upon me, and enemies on every side, and I realized that any effort then at escape would result in failure, and probably cause the death of all the prisoners.

Mrs. Larimer, with her boy, came to us, trembling with fear, saying, " The men have all escaped, and left us to the mercy of the savages."

In reply, I said, "I do hope they have. What benefit would it be to us, to have them here, to suffer this fear and danger with us? They would be killed, and then all hope of rescue for us would be at an end."

Her agitation was extreme. Her grief seemed to have reached its climax when she saw the Indians destroying her property, which consisted principally of such articles as belong to the Daguerrean art. She had indulged in high hopes of fortune from the prosecution of this art among the mining towns of Idaho. As she saw her chemicals, picture cases, and other property pertaining to her calling, being destroyed, she uttered such a wild despairing cry as brought the chief of the band to us, who, with gleaming knife, threatened to end all her further troubles in this world. The moment was a critical one for her. The Indians were flushed with an easy-won victory over a weak party; they had "tasted blood," and it needed but slight provocation for them to shed that even of defenseless women and children.

My own agony could be no less than that of my companion in misfortune. The loss of our worldy possessions, which were not inconsiderable, consisting of a large herd of cattle, and groceries, and goods of particular value in the mining regions, I gave no thought to. The possible fate of my husband; the dark, fearful future that loomed before myself and little Mary, for whose possible future I had more apprehension than for my own, were thoughts that flashed through my mind to the exclusion of all mere pecuniary considerations.

But my poor companion was in great danger, and perhaps it was a selfish thought of future loneliness in captivity which induced me to intercede that her life might be spared. I went to the side of the chief, and, assuming a cheerfulness I was very far from feeling, plead successfully for her life.

I endeavored in every way to propitiate our savage captor, but received no evidences of kindness or relenting that I could then understand. He did present me, however, a wreath of gay feathers from his own head, which I took, regarding it merely as an ornament, when in reality, as I afterward learned, it was a token of his favor and protection.

He then left us, to secure his own share of plunder, but we saw that we were surrounded by a special guard of armed men, and so gave up all struggle against what seemed an inevitable doom, and sat down upon the ground in despair.

I know now that night had come upon us while we sat there, and that darkness was closing the scene of desolation and death before their arrangements for departure were completed.

The first intimation we had that our immediate massacre was not intended, was a few articles of clothing presented by a young Indian, whose name was Wechela, who intimated that we would have need for them.

It was a pitiable sight to see the terrified looks of our helpless children, who clung to us for the protection we could not give. Mrs. Larimer was unconscious of the death of any of our party. I did not tell her what my eyes had seen, fearing that she could not endure it, but strove to encourage and enliven her, lest her excitement would hasten her death or excite the anger of our captors.

We both feared that when the Indians made their arrangements for departure we would be quickly disposed of by the scalping knife; or even should we escape for the time, we saw no prospect of release from bondage. Terror of the most appalling nature for the fate of the children possessed me, and all the horrors of Indian captivity that we had ever heard crowded on our minds with a new and fearful meaning—the slow fires, the pitiless knife, the poisoned arrows, the torture of famine, and a thousand nameless phantoms of agony passed before our troubled souls, filling us with fears so harrowing that the pangs of dissolution compared to them must have been relief.

It may be thought almost impossible in such a chaos of dread to collect the soul in prayer, but

> When woe is come, the soul is dumb
> That crieth not to God,

and the only respite we could claim from despair was the lifting of our trembling hearts upward to the God of mercy.

Those hours of misery can never be forgotten. We were oppressed by terrors we could not explain or realize. The sudden separation from those we loved and relied on; our own helplessness and the gloom of uncertainty that hung over the future—surely none can better testify to the worth of trust in God than those whose hope on earth seemed ended; and, faint and weak as our faith was, it saved us from utter desolation and the blackness of despair.

From among the confused mass of material of all kinds scattered about, the same young Indian, Wechela, brought me a pair of shoes; also a pair of little Mary's. He looked kindly as he laid these articles before me, intimating by his gestures that our lives were to be spared, and that we should have need of them and other clothing during our long march into captivity. He also brought me some books and letters, all of which I thankfully received. I readily conceived a plan to make good use of them, and secreted as many as I could about my clothing. I said to Mrs. Larimer, "If I can retain these papers and letters, and we are forced to travel with the Indians into their unknown country, I shall drop them at intervals along the way we are taken, as a guide, and trust in God that our friends may find and follow them to our rescue, or if an opportunity of escape offer, we will seize it, and by their help retrace our steps."

The property that the Indians could not carry with

them, they gathered into a pile and lighted. The light of the flames showed us the forms of our captors busily loading their horses and ours with plunder, and preparing to depart. When their arrangements were completed, they came to us and signified that we must accompany them, pointing to the horses they led up to us, and motioning for us to mount. The horse assigned to me was one that had belonged to Mr. Larimer, and was crippled in the back. This I endeavored to make them understand, but failed.

This was the first reliable assurance they gave us that our lives were not in immediate danger, and we received it gratefully, for with the prospect of life hope revived, and faith to believe that God had not forsaken us, and that we might yet be united to our friends, who never seemed dearer than when we were about to be carried into captivity by the hostile sons of the forest.

Many persons have since assured me that, to them, death would have been preferable to life with such prospects, saying that rather than have submitted to be carried away by savages, to a dark and doubtful doom, they would have taken their own lives. But it is only those who have looked over the dark abyss of death who know how the soul shrinks from meeting the unknown future.

Experience is a grand teacher, and we were then in her school, and learned that while hope offers the faintest token of refuge, we pause upon the fearful brink of eternity, and look back for rescue.

Mrs. Larimer had climbed into her saddle, her boy placed behind her on the same horse, and started on, accompanied by a party of Indians. I also climbed into my saddle, but was no sooner there than the horse fell to the ground, and I under him, thus increasing the bruises I had already received, and causing me great pain. This accident detained me some time in the rear. A dread of being separated from the only white woman in that awful wilderness filled me with horror.

Soon they had another horse saddled for me, and assisted me to mount him. I looked around for my little Mary. There she stoood, a poor helpless lamb, in the midst of blood-thirsty savages. I stretched out my arms for her imploringly. For a moment they hesitated; then, to my unspeakable joy, they yielded, and gave me my child. They then started on, leading my horse; they also gave me a rope that was fastened around the horse's under jaw.

The air was cool, and the sky was bright with the glitter of starlight. The water, as it fell over the rocks in the distance, came to our eager ears with a faint, pleasant murmur. All nature seemed peaceful and pitiless in its calm repose, unconscious of our desolate misery; the cry of night-birds and chirp of insects came with painful distinctness as we turned to leave the valley of Little Box Elder.

Straining my eyes, I sought to penetrate the shadows of the woods where our fugitive friends might be hid. The smoldering ruins of our property fell into ashes and the smoke faded away; night had covered the traces of confusion and struggle with her shrouding mantle, and all seemed quiet and unbroken peace.

I turned for a last look, and even the smoke was gone; the solemn trees, the rippling water, the soft night wind and the starlight, told no tale of the desolation and death that had gone before; and I rode on in my helpless condition, with my child clinging to me, without guide or support, save my trust in God.

CHAPTER V.

PLAN FOR LITTLE MARY'S ESCAPE—TORTURES OF UNCERTAINTY—
UNSUCCESSFUL ATTEMPT TO ESCAPE.

THE Indians left the scene of their cruel rapacity, traveling northward, chanting their monotonous war song. After a ride of two miles, through tall weeds and bushes, we left the bottom lands, and ascended some bluffs, and soon after came to a creek, which was easily forded, and where the Indians quenched their thirst.

The hills beyond began to be more difficult to ascend, and the gorges seemed fearfully deep, as we looked into the black shadows unrelieved by the feeble light of the stars.

In the darkness of our ride, I conceived a plan for the escape of little Mary.

I whispered in her childish ear, " Mary, we are only a few miles from our camp, and the stream we have crossed you can easily wade through. I have dropped letters on the way, you know, to guide our friends in the direction we have taken; they will guide you back again, and it may be your only chance of escape from destruction. Drop gently down, and lie on the ground for a little while, to avoid being seen; then retrace your steps, and may God in mercy go with you. If I can, I will follow you."

The child, whose judgment was remarkable for her age, readily acceded to this plan; her eye brightened and her young heart throbbed as she thought of its success.

Watching the opportunity, I dropped her gently, carefully, and unobserved, to the ground, and she lay there, while the Indians pursued their way, unconscious of their loss.

To portray my feelings upon this separation would be impossible. The agony I suffered was indescribable. I was firmly convinced that my course was wise—that I had given her the only chance of escape within my power; yet the terrible uncertainty of what her fate might be in the way before her, was almost unbearable.

I continued to think of it so deeply that at last I grew desperate, and resolved to follow her at every risk. Accordingly, watching an opportunity, I, too, slipped to the ground under the friendly cover of night, and the horse went on without its rider.

My plan was not successful. My flight was soon discovered, and the Indian wheeled around and rode back in my pursuit. Crouching in the undergrowth I might have escaped in the darkness, were it not for their cunning. Forming in a line of forty or fifty abreast, they actually covered the ground as they rode past me.

The horses themselves were thus led to betray me, for, being frightened at my crouching form, they stopped and reared, thus informing them of my hiding-place.

With great presence of mind I arose the moment I found myself discovered, and relating my story, the invention of an instant, I succeeded partially in allaying their anger.

I told them the child had fallen asleep and dropped from the horse; that I had endeavored to call their attention to it, but in vain; and, fearing I would be unable to find her if we rode further, I had jumped down and attempted the search alone.

The Indians used great violence toward me, assuring me that if any further attempts were made to escape, my punishment would be accordingly.

They then promised to send a party out in search of the child when it became light.

Poor little Mary! alone in the wilderness, a little, helpless child; who can portray her terror!

With faith to trust, and courage to dare, that little, trembling form through the long hours of the night kept watch.

The lonely cry of the night-bird had no fear in its melancholy scream for the little wanderer who crouched amid the prairie grass. The baying of the gray wolf, as he passed the lonely watcher, might startle, but could not drive the faith from her heart.

Surely God is just, and angels will guide the faltering feet to friends and home. Innocent of wrong, how could she but trust that the unseen hands of spirits would guide her from the surrounding perils!

A Scene on the Third Night after My Capture.

THE BUFFALO HUNT.

CHAPTER VI.

CONTINUATION OF OUR MARCH INTO THE WILDERNESS—SUFFERING
FROM THIRST AND WEARINESS—DISAPPEARANCE OF MY FELLOW
PRISONER—LOSS OF THE OLD CHIEF'S PIPE AND ITS CONSEQUENCES
TO ME—A SCENE OF TERROR.

To take up the thread of my own narrative again,
and the continuation of my journey with the savages,
after the never-to-be-forgotten night when I parted
with little Mary, and the attempt to escape myself, will
be to entertain my reader with a sight of the dangerous and precipitous paths among the great bluffs which
we had been approaching, and the dizzy, fearful heights
leading over the dark abyss, or the gloomy, terrible
gorge, where only an Indian dares to venture.

The blackness of night, and the dread of our savage
companions, added terror to this perilous ride. As we
passed the little creek before we plunged into these
rocky fastnesses, we had left some scattered woods along
its banks.

I remember looking longingly at the dim shelter of
these friendly trees, and being possessed by an almost
uncontrollable desire to leap from the horse and dare
my fate in endeavoring to reach their protecting shade;

but the Indians' rifles behind me, and my dread of instant death, restrained me. And now my attention was attracted by the wild and terrible scenery around us, through which our fearful captors rode at ease, although it seemed impossible for man or beast to retain a footing over such craggy peaks and through such rugged ravines.

The cool air and the sound of rippling water warned us of our nearness to a river; and soon the savages turned their horses down a steep declivity that, like a mighty wall, closed in the great bed of the North Platte.

I saw that the river was rapid and deep, but we crossed the sands, plunged in, and braved the current.

From the child to my husband was an easy transition; indeed, when I thought of one, the other was present in my mind; and to mark the path of our retreat with the letters and papers I dropped on our way, seemed the only hope I had of his being able to come to my rescue.

As the horses plunged into the swelling river I secretly dropped another letter, that, I prayed, might be a clue to the labyrinth through which we were being led; for I could see by all the Indians' precautions, that to mislead any who should have the temerity to attempt our recovery, was the design of their movements.

They had taken paths inaccessible to white men, and made their crossing at a point where it would be impossible for trains to pass, so that they might avoid meeting emigrants. Having reached the opposite bank they separated into squads, and started in every direction, except southward, so as to mislead or confuse pursuers by the various trails.

—The band that surrounded and directed us kept to the northward a little by west. I tried to keep the points of compass clearly, because it seemed part of the hope that sustained me.

Mr. Kelly had said that our position on the Little Box Elder was about twelve miles from Deer Creek Station, which lay to the northwest of us. Marking our present course, I tried, by calculating the distance, to keep that position in my mind, for toward it my yearning desire for help and relief turned.

After crossing the river and issuing from the bluffs we came to a bright, cool stream of water in a lovely valley, which ran through its bosom, spreading a delicious freshness all around.

Brilliant flowers opened their gorgeous cups to the coming sunshine, and delicate blossoms hid themselves among the rich shrubbery and at the mossy roots of grand old trees.

The awakening birds soared upward with loud and joyful melodies, and nature rejoiced at approaching day.

The beauty and loveliness of the scene mocked my sleepless eyes, and despair tugged at my heart-strings;

still I made superhuman efforts to appear cheerful, for
my only refuge was in being submissive and practicing
conciliation. My fear of them was too powerful to
allow me to give way to emotion for one moment.

There were sentinels stationed at different places to
give the alarm, in case of any one approaching to
rescue, and I afterward learned that in such a case I
would have been instantly murdered.

Next morning I learned, by signs, that Indians had
gone out in search of little Mary, scattering themselves
over the hills, in squads. Those remaining were constantly overlooking their plunder and unrolling bundles
taken from our wagons. They indulged their admiration for their spoils in loud conversation.

The Indians seemed to select, with a clear knowledge
of natural beauty, such localities as seemed best fitted
to suggest refreshment and repose.

The scenery through which we had passed was
wildly grand; it now became serenely beautiful, and to
a lover of nature, with a mind free from fear and
anxiety, the whole picture would have been a dream of
delight.

The night of my capture, I was ordered to lie down
on the ground, near a wounded Indian. A circle of
them guarded me, and three fierce warriors sat near me
with drawn tomahawks.

Reader, imagine my feelings, after the terrible scenes
of the day previous; the desolate white woman in the

power of revengeful savages, not daring to speak, lest their fury should fall on my defenceless head.

My great anxiety now was to preserve my sanity, which threatened to be overcome if I did not arouse myself to hope, and put aside the feeling of despair which at times stole over me. My heart was continually lifted to "Our Father," and confidently I now began to feel that prayer would be answered, and that God would deliver me in due season. This nerved me to endure and appear submissive.

At early dawn I was aroused from my apparent slumbers by the war chief, who sent me out to catch the horses—our American horses being afraid of the savages—and as the animals were those belonging to our train, it was supposed that I could do so readily.

Upon returning, my eyes were gladdened by the sight of my fellow prisoner, who was seated with her boy upon the ground, eating buffalo meat and crackers. I went immediately to her, and we conversed in low tones, telling her of my intention to escape the first opportunity. She seemed much depressed, but I endeavored to re-assure her, and bidding her hope for the best, went back to where the Indians were making ropes, and packing their goods and plunder more securely, preparatory to the succeding march, which was commenced at an early hour of the day.

We proceeded on our journey until near noon, when we halted in a valley not far to the north of Deer Creek

Station, and I met this lady again. It was a clear and beautiful valley where we rested, until the scorching rays of the sun had faded in the horizon.

Being burdened with the gun, and bow and arrow of the chief, my tired arms were relieved, and I plead for the privilege of camping here all night for many reasons. One was, we might be overtaken by friends sent to rescue us, and the distance of return would be less if I should be successful in my next attempt to escape.

My entreaties were unavailing; the savages were determined to go forward, and we were soon mounted and started on. We traveled until sunset, then camped for the night in a secluded valley; we seemed to enter this valley along the base of a wall, composed of bluffs or peaks. Within these circling hills it lay, a green, cool resting place, watered by a bright sparkling stream, and pleasantly dotted with bushes and undergrowth.

The moon wént down early, and in the dim, uncertain star light, the heavy bluffs seemed to shut us in on all sides, rising grimly, like guardians, over our imprisoned lines. Blankets were spread, and on these the Indians rested.

I was then led out some distance in the camp, and securely fastened for the night. But before this, I remarked, to my fellow prisoner, my determination to escape that night, if my life were the forfeit, as in every wind I fancied I could hear the voice of little Mary calling me. She entreated me not to leave her, but promising help to her should I be fortunate enough to get free, I sadly bade her good night, and went to my allotted place.

In the morning, when permitted to rise, I learned that she had disappeared. A terrible sense of isolation closed around me. No one can realize the sensation without in some measure experiencing it.

I was desolate before, but now that I knew myself separated from my only white companion, the feeling increased tenfold, and seemed to weigh me down with its awful gloomy horror.

In the heart of the wilderness, surrounded by creatures with whom no chord of sympathy was entertained—far from home, friends and the interests of civilized life—the attractions of society, and, above all, separated from husband and loved ones—there seemed but one glimpse of light, in all the blackness of despair, left, and that was flight.

I listened to every sound, while moments appeared hours, and it seemed to me that death in its most terrible form would not be so hard to bear as the torturing agony I then endured.

I murmured broken prayers. I seemed to hear the voices of my husband and child calling me, and springing forward, with a wild belief that it was real, would sink back again, overwhelmed with fresh agony.

Arrangements were then made for resuming our journey, and we were soon once more on our march.

Another burden had been added to my almost worn-out frame, the leading of an unruly horse; and my arms were so full of the implements I was forced to carry, that I threw away the pipe of the old chief—a tube nearly three feet long, and given me to take care of—which was very unfortunate for me, exciting the wrath and anger of the chief to a terrible degree.

Now they seemed to regard me with a suspicious aversion, and were not so kind as before.

The country they passed over was high, dry, and barren. I rode one horse and led another; and when evening came they stopped to rest in a grove of great timber, where there was a dry creek bed.

Water was obtained by digging in the sand, but the supply was meager, and I was allowed none.

The sun began to sink, and the chief was so enraged against me, that he told me by signs that I should behold it rise no more.

Grinding his teeth with wrathful anger, he made me understand that I was not to be trusted; had once tried to escape; had made them suffer the loss of my child, and that my life would be the forfeit.

A large fire had been built, and they all danced around it. Night had begun to darken heavily over me, and I stood trembling and horror struck, not knowing but that the flame the savages capered about was destined to consume my tortured form.

The pipe of the chief was nowhere to be found, and

it was demanded of me to produce it. He used the Indian words, "Chopa-chanopa," uttered in a voice of thunder, accompanying them with gestures, whose meaning was too threatening to be mistaken.

I looked in fear and dismay around me, utterly at a loss to know what was expected, yet dreading the consequences of failing to obey.

Wechela, the Indian boy, who had been so kind to me, now came up, and made the motion of puffing with his lips, to help me; and then I remembered that I had broken the pipe the day before, and thrown it away, ignorant of their veneration for the pipe, and of its value as a peace offering.

The chief declared that I should die for having caused the loss of his pipe.

An untamed horse was brought, and they told me I would be placed on it as a target for their deadliest arrows, and the animal might then run at will, carrying my body where it would.

Helpless, and almost dying with terror at my situation, I sank on a rocky seat in their midst. They were all armed, and anxiously awaited the signal. They had pistols, bows, and spears; and I noticed some stoop, and raise blazing fire-brands to frighten the pawing beast that was to bear me to death.

In speechless agony I raised my soul to God! Soon it would stand before his throne, and with all the pleading passion of my sinking soul I prayed for

pardon and favor in his precious blood, who had
suffered for my sins, and risen on high for my justifi-
cation.

In an instant a life-time of thought condensed itself
into my mind, and I could see my old home and hear
my mother's voice; and the contrast between the love
I had been so ruthlessly torn from, and the hundreds
of savage faces, gleaming with ferocity and excitement
around me, seemed like the lights and shadows of
some weird picture.

But I was to die, and I desired, with all the strength
of my soul, to grasp the promises of God's mercy, and
free my parting spirit from all revengeful, earthly
thoughts.

In what I almost felt my final breath, I prayed for
my own salvation, and the forgiveness of my enemies;
and remembering a purse of money which was in my
pocket, knowing that it would decay with my body in
the wilderness, I drew it out, and, with suffused eyes,
divided it among them, though my hands were growing powerless and my sight failing. One hundred and
twenty dollars in notes I gave them, telling them its
value as I did so, when, to my astonishment, a change
came over their faces. They laid their weapons on the
ground, seemingly pleased, and anxious to understand,
requesting me to explain the worth of each note
clearly, by holding up my fingers.

Eagerly I tried to obey, perceiving the hope their

milder manner held out; but my cold hands fell powerless by my side, my tongue refused to utter a sound, and, unconsciously, I sank to the ground utterly insensible to objects around me.

When insensibility gave way to returning feeling, I was still on the ground where I had fallen, but preparations for the deadly scene were gone, and the savages slumbered on the ground near me by the faint firelight. Crawling into a sitting posture, I surveyed the camp, and saw hundreds of sleeping forms lying in groups around, with watches set in their places, and no opportunity to escape, even if strength permitted.

Weak and trembling, I sank down, and lay silent till day-break, when the camp was again put in motion, and, at their bidding, I mounted one horse and led another, as I had done on the day previous.

This was no easy task, for the pack-horse, which had not been broken, would frequently pull back so violently as to bring me to the ground, at which the chief would become fearfully angry, threatening to kill me at once.

Practicing great caution, and using strong effort, I would strive to remain in the saddle to avoid the cuffs and blows received.

Whenever the bridle would slip inadvertently from my hand, the chief's blasphemous language would all be English; a sad commentary on the benefits white men confer on their savage brethren when brought into close contact.

Drunkenness, profanity, and dissolute habits are the lessons of civilization to the red men, and when the weapons we furnish are turned against ourselves, their edge is keen indeed.

Feeling that I had forfeited the good will of the Indians, and knowing that the tenure of my life was most uncertain, I dared make no complaint, although hunger and devouring thirst tortured me.

The way still led through dry and sandy hills, upon which the sun glared down with exhausting heat, and seemed to scorch life and moisture out of all his rays fell upon. As far as my eye could reach, nothing but burning sand, and withering sage brush or thorny cactus, was to be seen. All my surroundings only served to aggravate the thirst which the terrible heat of that long day's ride increased to frenzy.

When, in famishing despair I closed my eyes, a cup of cool, delicious drink would seem to be presented to my lips, only to be cruelly withdrawn; and this torture seemed to me like the agony of the rich man, who besought Lazarus for one drop of water to cool his parched tongue.

I thought of all I had been separated from, as it seemed to me, forever, and the torment of the hour reduced me to despair. I wished to die, feeling that the pangs of dissolution could not surpass the anguish of my living death. My voice was almost gone, and with difficulty I maintained my seat in the saddle.

Turning my eyes despairingly to my captors, I uttered the word " Minne," signifying water in their language, and kept repeating it imploringly at intervals. They seemed to hurry forward, and, just at sunset, came in sight of a grassy valley through which flowed a river, and the sight of it came like hope to my almost dying eyes.

A little brook from the hills above found its way into the waters of this greater stream, and here they dismounted, and, lifting me from my horse, laid me in its shallow bed. I had become almost unconscious, and the cool, delightful element revived me. At first I was not able to drink, but gradually my strength renewed itself, and I found relief from the indescribable pangs of thirst.

The stream by which the Indians camped that night was Powder River; and here, in 1866, Fort Conner was built, which in the following year was named Fort Reno.

CHAPTER VII.

POWDER RIVER—ANOTHER ATTEMPT TO ESCAPE—DETECTION AND
DESPAIR—A QUARREL—MY LIFE SAVED BY "JUMPING BEAR."

THE name given to Powder River by the Indians, is
"Chahalee Wacapolah." It crosses the country east of
the Big Horn Mountains, and from its banks can be
seen the snow-capped Cloud Peak rising grandly from
its surrounding hills. Between these ranges, that cul-
minate in the queenly, shining crowned height that
takes its name from the clouds it seems to pierce, are
fertile valleys, in which game abounds, and delicious
wild fruits in great variety, some of which can not be
surpassed by cultivated orchard products in the richness and flavor they possess, although they ripen in
the neighborhood of everlasting snow.

In these valleys the country seems to roll in gentle
slopes, presenting to the eye many elements of loveliness and future value.

Powder River, which is a muddy stream, comes
from the southern side of the Big Horn Mountains,
and takes a southwestern course, and therefore is not
a part of the bright channel that combines to feed the
Missouri River from the Big Horn range.

This range of the Rocky Mountains possesses two distinct, marked features. First, there is a central or back-bone range, which culminates in perpetual snow, where Cloud Peak grandly rises, as the chief of all its proud summits. Falling off gradually toward the southern valley, there are similar ranges of the Wind River Mountains beyond.

Between these ranges, and varying in breadth from twelve to twenty-five miles, are fine hunting grounds, abounding in noble orchards of wild fruit of various kinds, and grapes, as well as game of the choicest kind for the huntsman. Notwithstanding its vicinity to snow, there are gentle slopes which present features of peculiar loveliness.

Several miles northwest, and following the sweep of the higher northern range, and six to eight miles outside its general base, a new country opens. Sage brush and cactus, which for nearly two hundred miles have so largely monopolized the soil, rapidly disappear.

The change, though sudden, is very beautiful. One narrow divide only is crossed, and the transition about one day's ride from the above-named river. The limpid, transparent, and noisy waters of Deer Fork are reached, and the horses have difficulty in breasting the swift current. The river is so clear that every pebble and fish is seen distinctly on the bottom, and the water so cool that ice in midsummer is no object of desire.

The scenes of natural beauty, and the charms that

have endeared this country to the savage, will in the future lure the emigrant seeking a home in this new and undeveloped land.

This clear creek is a genuine outflow from the Big Horn Mountains, and is a type of many others, no less pure and valuable, derived from melting snow and from innumerable springs in the mountains.

Rock Creek comes next, with far less pretensions, but is similar in character.

A day's ride to the northward brings the traveler to Crazy Woman's Fork.

This ever-flowing stream receives its yellow hue from the Powder River waters, of which it is a branch.

The country is scarred by countless trails of buffalo, so that what is often called the Indian trail is merely the hoof-print of these animals.

Leaving Powder River, we passed through large pine forests, and through valleys rich with beautiful grasses, with limpid springs and seemingly eternal verdure.

I continued to drop papers by the way, hoping they might lead to my discovery, which would have proved fatal had any one attempted a rescue, as the Indians prefer to kill their captives rather than be forced to give them up.

It was the fifth night of my sojourn with the Indians that I found myself under the weeping willows of Clear Creek.

The men, weary with travel, and glad to find so good a camping ground, lay down to sleep, leaving a sufficient guard over their captive and at the outposts.

Their journey hither had been a perilous one to me, unused as I was to the rocky paths between narrow gorges and over masses of broken stone, which their Indian ponies climbed with readiness and ease.

I was led to remark the difference between these ponies and American horses, who could only struggle to find their foothold over such craggy ground, while the ponies led the way, picking their steps up almost perpendicular steeps with burdens on their backs.

Their travel after the rest at Clear Creek partook of the difficult nature of the mountain passes, and was wearisome in the extreme, and the duties imposed upon me made life almost too burdensome to be borne. I was always glad of a respite at the camping ground.

On the sixth night, I lay on a rock, under the shade of some bushes, meditating on the possibility of escape.

The way was far beyond my reckoning, and the woods where they now were might be infested with wild beasts; but the prospect of getting away, and being free from the savages, closed my eyes to the terrors of starvation and ravenous animals.

Softly I rose and attempted to steal toward some growing timber; but the watchful chief did not risk his prey so carelessly, his keen eye was on me, and his iron hand grasped my wrist and drew me back.

Throwing me fiercely on the ground, he hissed a threat through his clenched teeth, which I momentarily expected him to put into execution, as I lay trembling at his feet.

I felt from this time that my captivity was for life, and a dull despair took possession of me.

Sleep, that balm for happier souls, brought only horrid dreams, in which a dreadful future pictured itself; and then the voices of my husband and child seemed calling me to their side, alas! in vain, for when I awoke it was to find myself in the grass of the savage camping ground, watched over by the relentless guard, and shut out from hope of home or civilized life.

My feet were covered with a pair of good shoes, and the chief's brother-in-law gave me a pair of stockings from his stores, which I gladly accepted, never, for a moment, suspecting that, in doing thus, I was outraging a custom of the people among whom I was.

The chief saw the gift, and made no remark at the time, but soon after he shot one of his brother-in-law's horses, which he objected to in a decided manner, and a quarrel ensued.

Realizing that I was the cause of the disagreement, I tremblingly watched the contest, unable to conciliate either combatant, and dreading the wrath of both.

The chief would brook no interference, nor would he offer any reparation for the wrong he had inflicted.

His brother-in-law, enraged at his arrogance, drew

his bow, and aimed his arrow at my heart, determined
to have satisfaction for the loss of his horse.

I could only cry to God for mercy, and prepare to
meet the death which had long hung over my head,
when a young Blackfoot, whose name was Jumping
Bear, saved me from the approaching doom by dexter-
ously snatching the bow from the savage and hurling
it to the earth.

He was named Jumping Bear from the almost miraculous dexterity of some of his feats.

This circumstance and the Indian mentioned were,
in my judgment, instruments in the hand of Providence, in saving Fort Sully from the vengeance and
slaughter of the Blackfeet, who had succeeded in gaining the confidence of some of the officers on the Missouri River.

His activity in the attack on our train, and the
energy he displayed in killing and pillaging on that
occasion, notwithstanding his efforts to make me believe
the contrary, forbade me to think there was any sympathy in his interference in my behalf.

The Indian submitted to his intervention so far that
he did not draw his bow again, and my suspense was
relieved, for the time, by the gift of a horse from the
chief to his brother-in-law, which calmed the fury of
the wronged Indian.

It happened that the animal thus given as a peace-
offering was the pack horse that pulled so uncomfort-

ably against the leading rein, and thus, in the end, I gained, by the ordeal through which I had passed, in being relieved of a most unmanageable task.

From the first, I was deprived of every ameliorating comfort that might have rendered my existence bearable.

No tent was spread for me, no rug, or coverlet, offered me to lie on. The hard earth, sparsely spread with grass, furnished me a couch, and apprehension and regret deprived me of the rest my toilsome life demanded. They offered me no food, and at first I did not dare to ask for it.

This was partly owing to the absence of all natural appetite, an intense weakness and craving constantly for drink being the only signs of the prolonged fast that annoyed me.

The utter hopelessness of my isolation wore on me, driving me almost to madness, and visions of husband and child haunted my brain; sometimes they were full of hope and tauntingly happy; at others, I saw them dying or dead, but always beyond my reach, and separated by the impassable barrier of my probably life-long captivity.

In my weakened condition, the horrors of the stake, to which I felt myself borne daily nearer as they progressed on their homeward route, appeared like a horrid phantom.

It had been threatened me since my first effort to

escape, and I was led to believe such a punishment was the inevitable consequence of my attempt.

The terrible heat of the days continued, and the road they took was singularly barren of water. The Indians, after drinking plentifully before starting, carry little sticks in their mouths, which they chew constantly, thus creating saliva, and preventing the parching sensation I endured from the want of this knowledge.

The seventh night they entered a singular cañon, apparently well known to them, as they found horses there, which evidently had been left on a former visit.

I could not but wonder at the sagacity and patience of these Indian ponies, which were content to wait their master's coming, and browse about on the sparse herbage and meager grass.

The Indians had killed an antelope that day, and a piece of the raw flesh was allotted me for a meal. They had then traveled in a circuitous route for miles, to reach the mouth of this cañon, and entered it just after sundown.

Its gloomy shade was a great relief after the heat of the sun, and it filled my sensitive mind with awe. The sun never seemed to penetrate its depths, and the damp air rose around me like the breath of a dungeon.

Downward they went, as if descending into the bowels of the earth, and the sloping floor they trod was covered with red sand for perhaps the space of half a mile.

Then they struck a rocky pavement, the perpendicular walls of which were of earth; but as they made another turning and entered a large space, they seemed to change to stone with projecting arches and overhanging cornices.

The high walls rose above the base so as to nearly meet overhead, and, with their innumerable juttings and irregularities, had the appearance of carved columns supporting a mighty ruin.

Occasionally a faint ray of the fading light struggled with the gloom, into which they plunged deeper and deeper, and then their horses' cautious feet would turn the bones of antelope or deer, drawn thither by the lurking wolf to feed the young in their lair.

I was startled with dread at the sight, fearing that they might be human bones, with which mine would soon be mingled.

The increasing darkness had made it necessary for the Indians to carry torches, which they did, lighting up the grotesque grandeur of earth and rock through which they passed by the weird glare of their waving brands.

Arriving at the spot they selected as a camping-ground, they made fires, whose fantastic gleams danced upon the rocky walls, and added a magic splendor to their wondrous tracery. The ghostly grandeur of these unfrequented shades can not be described, but their effect is marvelous.

They seem to shadow forth the outline of carving and sculpture, and in the uncertain fire-light have all the effect of some old-time temple, whose art and glory will live forever, even when its classic stones are dust.

Here I found water for my parched lips, which was more grateful to my weary senses than any natural phenomenon; and sinking on a moss-grown rock, near the trickling rill that sank away in the sand beyond, I found slumber in that strange, fantastic solitude.

I was aroused by a whistling sound, and, gathering myself up, looked fearfully around me. Two flaming eyes seemed to pierce the darkness like a sword. I shuddered and held my breath, as a long, lithe serpent wound past me, trailing its shining length through the damp sand, and moving slowly out of sight among the dripping vines.

After that I slept no more; and when I saw the struggling light of day pierce the rocky opening above, I gladly hailed the safety of the sunshine, even though it brought sorrow, distress, and toil.

When we rose in the morning, they left the cañon by the path they entered, as it seemed to have no other outlet, and then pursued their way.

CHAPTER VIII.

THE STORM—ARRIVAL AT THE INDIAN VILLAGE—THE OLD CHIEF'S
WIFE—SOME KINDNESS SHOWN ME—ATTEND A FEAST.

ON the 20th of July we had nearly reached the Indian village, when we camped for the night, as usual, when such a locality could be gained, on the bank of a stream of good water.

Here was a stream of sparkling, rippling water, fresh from the melting snow of the mountain. It was a warm, still night. Soon the sky began to darken strangely, and great ragged masses of clouds hung low over the surrounding hills. The air grew heavy, relieved occasionally by a deep gust of wind, that died away, to be succeeded by an ominous calm. Then a low, muttering thunder jarred painfully on the ear. My shattered nerves recoiled at the prospect of the coming storm. From a child I had been timid of lightning, and now its forked gleam filled me with dismay in my unsheltered helplessness.

The Indians, seeing the approaching tempest, prepared for it by collecting and fastening their horses, and covering their fire-arms and amunition, and lying flat on the earth themselves. I crouched, too, but could not escape the terrible glare of the lightning, and the roar of the awful thunder grew deafening.

On came the storm with startling velocity, and the dread artillery of heaven boomed overhead, followed closely by blinding flashes of light; and the velocity of the whirlwind seemed to arise in its might, to add desolation to the terrible scene.

When the vivid gleams lit up the air, enormous trees could be seen bending under the fierceness of the blast, and great white sheets of water burst out of the clouds, as if intent on deluging the world. Every element in nature united in terrific warfare, and the security of earth seemed denied to me while I clung to its flooded bosom, and, blinded by lightning and shocked by the incessant roaring of the thunder and the wild ravaging of the ungovernable wind, felt myself but a tossed atom in the great confusion, and could only cling to God's remembering pity in silent prayer.

Huge trees were bent to the earth and broken; others, snapped off like twigs, were carried through the frenzied air. Some forest monarchs were left bare of leaves or boughs, like desolate old age stripped of its honors.

The rain had already swelled the little creek into a mighty stream, that rolled its dark, angry waters with fury, and added its sullen roar to the howlings of the storm. I screamed, but my voice was lost even to

myself in the mightier ones of the furious elements.
Three hours—three long, never-to-be-forgotten hours—
did the storm rage thus in fury, and in those hours I
thought I lived a life-time! Then, to my joy, it began to abate, and soon I beheld the twinkling stars
through rents in the driving clouds, while the flashing
lightning and the roaring thunders gradually becoming less and less distinct to the eye and ear, told me
the devastating storm was speeding on toward the
east; and when, at dawn of day, the waters were as-
suaged, the thunder died away, and the lightnings
were chained in their cell, the scene was one of indescribable desolation. The wind had gone home; daylight had cowed him from a raging giant into a meek
prisoner, and led him moaning to his cavern in the
eastern hills. A strangely-solemn calm seemed to
take the place of the wild conflict; but the track of
destruction was there, and the swollen water and
felled trees, the scattered boughs and uprooted sap-
lings, told the story of the havoc of the storm.

It was a night of horror to pass through, and I
thankfully greeted the returning day, that once more
gave me the comfort of light, now almost my only
solace, for my position grew more bitter, as the chief's
savage-like exultation in my capture and safe abduc-
tion increased as we neared the village where their
families were, and where I feared my fate would be
decided by bloodshed or the fearful stake.

On the 21st of July we left camp early, the day being cool and favorable for traveling. Our route lay over rolling prairie, interspersed with extensive tracts of marsh, which, however, we easily avoided crossing. A few miles brought us to a high, broken ridge, stretching nearly in a north and south direction. As we ascended the ridge we came in sight of a large herd of buffalo, quietly feeding upon the bunch, or buffalo grass, which they prefer to all other kinds. These animals are short-sighted, and scent the approach of an enemy before they can see him, and thus, in their curiosity, often start to meet him, until they approach near enough to ascertain to their satisfaction whether there be danger in a closer acquaintance. In this case they decided in the affirmative, and, when they had once fairly made us out, lost no time in increasing the distance between us, starting on a slow, clumsy trot, which was soon quickened to a gait that generally left most pursuers far in the rear.

But the Indians and their horses both are trained buffalo hunters, and soon succeeded in surrounding a number. They ride alongside their victim, and, leveling their guns or arrows, send their aimed shot in the region of the heart, then ride off to a safe distance, to avoid the desperate lunge which a wounded buffalo seldom fails to make, and, shaking his shaggy head, crowned with horns of most formidable strength, stands at bay, with eyes darting, savage and defiant, as he looks at his human foe. Soon the blood begins to spirt from his mouth, and to choke him as it comes. The hunters do not shoot again, but wait patiently until their victim grows weak from loss of blood, and, staggering, falls upon his knees, makes a desperate effort to regain his feet, and get at his slayer, then falling once more, rolls over on his side, dead.

Sometimes these animals number tens of thousands, in droves. The Indians often, for the mere sport, make an onslaught, killing great numbers of them, and having a plentiful feast of " ta-tonka," as they call buffalo meat. They use no economy in food. It is always a feast or a famine; and they seem equally able to gorge or fast. Each man selects the part of the animal he has killed that best suits his own taste, and leaves the rest to decay or be eaten by wolves, thus wasting their own game, and often suffering privation in consequence.

They gave me a knife and motioned me to help myself to the feast. I did not accept, thinking then it would never be possible for me to eat uncooked meat.

They remained here over night, starting early next morning. We were now nearing the village where the Indians belonged.

Jumping Bear, the young Indian who had shown me so many marks of good will, again made his appearance, with a sad expression on his face, and that day would ride in silence by my side; which was an act of great condescension on his part, for these men rarely thus equalize themselves with women, but ride in advance.

They had traveled nearly three hundred miles, and, despite my fears, I began to rejoice in the prospect of arriving among women, even though they were savages; and a dawning hope that I might find pity and companionship with beings of my own sex, however separated their lives and customs might be, took posssesion of me.

I had read of the dusky maidens of romance; I thought of all the characters of romance and history, wherein the nature of the red man is enshrined in poetic beauty. The untutored nobility of soul, the brave generosity, the simple dignity untrammelled by the hollow conventionalities of civilized life, all rose mockingly before me, and the heroes of my youthful imagination passed through my mind in strange contrast with the flesh and blood realities into whose hands I had fallen.

The stately Logan, the fearless Philip, the bold Black Hawk, the gentle Pocahontas: how unlike the greedy, cunning and cruel savages who had so ruthlessly torn me from my friends!

Truly, those pictures of the children of the forest that adorn the pages of the novelist are delightful conceptions of the airy fancy, fitted to charm the mind. They amuse and beguile the hours they invest with their interest; but the true red man, as I saw him, does not exist between the pages of many volumes. He roams his native wastes, and to once encounter and study him there, so much must be sacrificed that I could scarcely appreciate the knowledge I was gaining at such a price.

Notwithstanding all I had seen and experienced, I remembered much that was gentle and faithful in the character ascribed to the Indian women. Perhaps I might be able to find one whose sympathy and companionship could be wrought upon to the extent of aiding me in some way to escape. I became hopeful with the thought, and almost forgot my terror of the threats of my captors, in my desire to see the friendly faces of Indian women.

The country around was rich and varied. Beautiful birds appeared in the trees, and flowers of variety and fragrance nodded on their stems. Wild fruits were abundant, and I plucked roses and fruit for food, while my savage companions feasted on raw meat. They did not seem to care for fruit, and urged me to eat meat with them. I refused, because of its being raw. A young Indian, guessing the cause of my refusal to eat, procured a kettle, made a fire, cooked some, and offered it to me. I tried to eat of it to please them, since they had taken the trouble to prepare a special dish, but owing to the filthy manner in which it was prepared a very small portion satisfied me.

We were now nearing a river, which, from its locality, must have been the Tongue River, where we found refreshing drink, and rested for a short time. The Indians gave me to understand that when we crossed this stream, and a short distance beyond, we would be at their home.

Here they paused to dress, so as to make a gay appearance and imposing entrance into the village. Except when in full dress, an Indian's wearing apparel consists only of a buffalo robe, which is also part of a fine toilet. It is very inconveniently disposed about the person, without fastening, and must be held in position with the hands.

Here the clothing taken from our train was brought into great demand, and each warrior that had been fortunate enough to possess himself of any article of our dress, now arrayed himself to the best advantage the garments and their limited ideas of civilization permitted; and, in some instances, when the toilet was considered complete, changes for less attractive articles of display were made with companions who had not been so fortunate as others in the division of the goods, that they might also share in the sport afforded by this derisive display.

Their peculiar ideas of tasteful dress rendered them grotesque in appearance. One brawny face appeared under the shade of my hat, smiling with evident satisfaction at the superiority of his decorations over those of his less fortunate companions; another was shaded from the scorching rays of the sun by a tiny parasol, and the brown hand that held it aloft was thinly covered by a silk glove, which was about the only article of clothing, except the invariable breech-cloth, that the warrior wore.

Vests and other garments were put on with the lower part upward; and they all displayed remarkable fertility in the arrangement of their decorations. They seemed to think much of their stolen goods, some of which were frivolous, and others worthless.

Decorating themselves by way of derision, each noble warrior endeavored to outdo the other in splendor, which was altogether estimated by color, and not by texture. Their horses were also decked in the most ridiculous manner.

Ottawa, or Silver Horn, the war chief, was arrayed in full costume. He was very old, over seventy-five, partially blind, and a little below the medium height. He was very ferocious and savage looking, and now, when in costume, looked frightful. His face was red, with stripes of black, and around each eye a circlet of bright yellow. His long, black hair was divided into two braids, with a scalp-lock on top of the head. His ears held great brass wire rings, full six inches in diameter, and chains and bead necklaces were suspended from his neck; armlets and bracelets of brass, together with a string of bears' claws, completed his jewelry. He wore also leggings of deer skin, and a shirt of the same material, beautifully ornamented with beads, and fringed with scalp-locks, that he claimed to have taken from his enemies, both red and white. Over his shoulders hung a great, bright-colored quilt, that had been taken from our stores. He wore a crown of eagle feathers on his head; also a plume of feathers depending from the back of the crown.

His horse, a noble-looking animal, was no less gorgeously arrayed. His ears were pierced, like his master's, and his neck was encircled by a wreath of bears' claws, taken from animals that the chief had slain. Some bells and a human scalp hung from his mane, forming together, thus arrayed, a museum of the trophies of the old chief's prowess on the war path, and of skill in the chase.

When all was arranged, the chief mounted his horse and rode on in triumph toward the village, highly elated over the possession of his white captive, whom he never looked back at or deigned to notice, except to chastise on account of her slowness, which was unavoidable, as I rode a jaded horse, and could not keep pace.

The entire Indian village poured forth to meet us, amid song and wild dancing, in the most enthusiastic manner, flourishing flags and weapons of war in frenzied joy as we entered the village, which, stretched for miles along the banks of the stream, resembled a vast military encampment, with the wigwams covered with white skins, like Sibley tents in shape and size, ranged without regard to order, but facing one point of the compass.

We penetrated through the irregular settlement for over a mile, accompanied by the enthusiastic escort of men, women, and children.

We rode in the center of a double column of Indians and directly in the rear of the chief, till we reached the door of his lodge, when several of his wives came out to meet him. He had six, but the senior one remained in the tent, while a younger one was absent with the Farmer or Grosventre Indians. Their salutation is very much in the manner of the Mexicans; the women crossed their arms on the chief's breast, and smiled.

They met me in silence, but with looks of great astonishment.

I got down as directed, and followed the chief into the great lodge or tent, distinguished from the others by its superior ornaments. It was decorated with brilliantly colored porcupine quills and a terrible fringe of human scalp-locks, taken in battle from the Pawnees.

On one side was depicted a representation of the Good Spirit, rude in design, and daubed with colors. On the other side was portrayed the figure of the spirit of evil in like manner. The Indians believe in these two deities and pay their homage to them. The first they consider as entirely benevolent and kind; but the second is full of vile tricks and wicked ways.

They fear him, and consider it only safe to propitiate him occasionally by obedience to his evil will. This may account for some of their worst ferocities, and explain that horrible brutality of nature which they so often exhibit.

The senior wife, who had remained in the lodge, met her husband with the same salutation as the others had done.

I was shown a seat opposite the entrance on a buffalo skin. The chief's spoil was brought in for division by his elderly spouse.

As it was spread out before them, the women gathered admiringly round it, and proved their peculiarities of taste; and love of finery had a counterpart in these forest belles, as well defined as if they had been city ladies. Eagerly they watched every new article displayed, grunting their approval, until their senior companion seized a piece of cloth, declaring that she meant to retain it all for herself.

This occasioned dissatisfaction, which soon ripened to rebellion among them, and they contended for a just distribution of the goods. The elder matron, following her illustrious husband's plan in quelling such outbreaks, caught her knife from her belt, sprang in among them, vowing that she was the oldest and had the right to govern, and threatening to kill every one if there was the least objection offered to her decrees. I had so hoped to find sympathy and pity among these artless women of the forest, but instead, cowed and trembling, I sat, scarcely daring to breathe.

The chief noticed my fear and shrinking posture, and smiled. Then he rose, and made a speech, which had its effect. The women became quiet. Presently an invitation arrived for the chief to go to a feast, and he rose to comply.

I followed his departing figure with regretful glances, for, terrible as he and his men had been, the women seemed still more formidable, and I feared to be left alone with them, especially with the hot temper and ready knife of the elder squaw.

Great crowds of curious Indians came flocking in to stare at me. The women brought their children. Some of them, whose fair complexion astonished me, I afterward learned were the offspring of fort marriages.

One fair little boy, who, with his mother, had just returned from Fort Laramie, came close to me. Finding the squaw could speak a few words in English, I addressed her, and was told, in reply to my questions, that she had been the wife of a captain there, but that his white wife arriving from the East, his Indian wife was told to return to her people; she did so, taking her child with her. The little boy was dressed completely in military clothes, even to the stripe on his pantaloons, and was a very bright, attractive child of about four years.

It was a very sad thought for me to realize that a parent could part with such a child, committing it forever to live in barbarous ignorance, and rove the woods among savages with the impress of his own superior race, so strongly mingled with his Indian origin. I saw many other fair-faced little children, and heard the sad story from their mothers, and was deeply pained to see their pale, pinched features, as they cried for food when there was none to be had; and they are sometimes cruelly treated by the full-blooded and larger children on account of their unfortunate birth.

Now that the question of property was decided between the women of the chief's family, they seemed kindly disposed toward me, and one of them brought me a dish of meat; many others followed her example, even from the neighboring lodges, and really seemed to pity me, and showed great evidences of compassion, and tried to express their sympathy in signs, because I had been torn from my own people, and compelled to come such a long fatiguing journey, and examined me all over and over again, and all about my dress, hands, and feet particularly. Then, to their great surprise, they discovered my bruised and almost broken limbs that occurred when first taken, also from the fall of the horse the first night of my captivity, and proceeded at once to dress my wounds.

I was just beginning to rejoice in the dawning kindness that seemed to soften their swarthy faces, when a messenger from the war chief arrived, accompanied by a small party of young warriors sent to conduct me to the chief's presence. I did not at first comprehend the summons, and, as every fresh announcement only awakened new fears, I dreaded to comply, yet dared not refuse. Seeing my hesitation, the senior wife allowed a little daughter of the chief's, whose name was Yellow Bird, to accompany me, and I was then conducted to several feasts, at each of which I was received with kindness, and promised good will and protection. It was here that the chief himself first condescended to speak kindly to me, and this and the companionship of the child Yellow Bird, who seemed to approach me with a trusting grace and freedom unlike the scared shyness of Indian children generally, inspired hope.

The chief here told me that henceforth I could call Yellow Bird my own, to take the place of my little girl that had been killed. I did not at once comprehend all of his meaning, still it gave me some hope of security.

When at nightfall we returned to the lodge, which, they told me, I must henceforth regard as home, I found the elder women busily pounding a post into the ground, and my fears were at once aroused, being always ready to take alarm, and suggested to me that it betokened some evil. On the contrary, it was simply some household arrangement of her own, for presently, putting on a camp kettle, she built a fire, and caused water to boil, and drew a tea, of which she gave me a portion, assuring me that it would cure the tired and weary feeling and secure me a good rest.

This proved true. Soon a deep drowsiness began to steal over the weary captive. My bed of furs was shown me. Yellow Bird was told to share my couch with me, and from this time on she was my constant attendant. I laid down, and the wife of the chief tenderly removed my moccasins, and I slept sweetly— the first true sleep I had enjoyed in many weary nights.

Before my eyes closed in slumber, my heart rose in gratitude unspeakable to God for his great and immeasurable mercy.

I readily adapted myself to my new position. The chief's three sisters shared the lodge with us.

The following day commenced my labors, and the chief's wife seemed to feel a protecting interest in me.

The day of the 25th of July was observed by continual feasting in honor of the safe return of the braves.

There was a large tent made by putting several together, where all the chiefs, medicine-men, and great warriors met for consultation and feasting. I was invited to attend, and was given an elevated seat, while the rest of the company all sat upon the ground, and mostly cross-legged, preparatory to the feast being dealt out.

In the center of the circle was erected a flag-staff, with many scalps, trophies, and ornaments fastened to it. Near the foot of the flag-staff were placed, in a row on the ground, several large kettles, in which was prepared the feast. Near the kettles on the ground, also, were a number of wooden bowls, in which the meat was to be served out. And in front, two or three women, who were there placed as waiters, to light the pipes for smoking, and also to deal out the food.

In these positions things stood, and all sat with thousands climbing and crowding around for a peep at me, as I appeared at the grand feast and council, when at length the chief arose, in a very handsome costume, and addressed the audience, and in his speech often pointed to me. I could understand but little of his meaning.

Several others also made speeches, that all sounded the same to me. I sat trembling with fear at these strange proceedings, fearing they were deliberating upon a plan of putting me to some cruel death to finish their amusement. It is impossible to describe my feelings on that day, as I sat in the midst of those wild, savage people. Soon a handsome pipe was lit and brought to the chief to smoke. He took it, and after presenting the stem to the north, the south, the east, and the west, and then to the sun that was over his head, uttered a few words, drew a few whiffs, then passed it around through the whole group, who all smoked. This smoking was conducted with the strictest adherence to exact and established form, and the feast throughout was conducted in the most positive silence.

The lids were raised from the kettles, which were all filled with dog's meat alone, it being well cooked and made into a sort of stew. Each guest had a large wooden bowl placed before him, with a quantity of dog's flesh floating in a profusion of soup or rich gravy, with a large spoon resting in the dish, made of buffalo horn.

In this most difficult and painful dilemma I sat, witnessing the solemnity; my dish was given me, and the absolute necessity of eating it was painful to contemplate. I tasted it a few times after much urging, and then resigned my dish, which was taken and passed around with others to every part of the group, who all ate heartily. In this way the feast ended, and all retired silently and gradually, until the ground was left to the waiters, who seemed to have charge of it during the whole occasion.

The women signified to me that I should feel highly honored by being called to feast with chiefs and great warriors; and seeing the spirit in which it was given, I could not but treat it respectfully, and receive it as a very high and marked compliment.

Since I witnessed it on this occasion, I have been

honored with numerous entertainments of the kind, and all conducted in the same solemn and impressive manner.

As far as I could see and understand, I feel authorized to pronounce the dog-feast a truly religious ceremony, wherein the superstitious Indian sees fit to sacrifice his faithful companion to bear testimony to the sacredness of his vows of friendship for the Great Spirit. He always offers up a portion of the meat to his deity, then puts it on the ground to remind him of the sacrifice and solemnity of the offering.

The dog, among all Indian tribes, is more esteemed and more valued than among any part of the civilized world. The Indian has more time to devote to his company, and his untutored mind more nearly assimilates to the nature of his faithful servant.

The flesh of these dogs, though apparently relished by the Indians, is undoubtedly inferior to venison and buffalo meat, of which feasts are constantly made, where friends are invited, as they are in civilized society, to a pleasant and convivial party; from which fact alone, it would seem clear that they have some extraordinary motive, at all events, for feasting on the flesh of that useful and faithful animal, even when as in the instance I have been describing.

Their village was well supplied with fresh and dried meat of the buffalo and deer. The dog-feast is given, I believe, by all tribes of America, and by them all,

I think, this faithful animal, as well as the horse, is sacrificed, in several different ways, to appease offended spirits or deities, whom it is considered necessary that they should conciliate in this way, and when done, is invariably done by giving the best in the herd or the kennel.

That night was spent in dancing. Wild and furious all seemed to me. I was led into the center of the circle, and assigned the painful duty of holding above my head human scalps fastened to a little pole. The dance was kept up until near morning, when all repaired to their respective lodges. The three kind sisters of the chief were there to convey me to mine.

CHAPTER IX.

THE next morning the whole village was in motion.
The warriors were going to battle against a white enemy, they said, and old men, women, and children
were sent out in another direction to a place of safety,
as designated by the chief. Every thing was soon
moving. With the rapidity of custom the tent-poles
were lowered and the tents rolled up. The cooking
utensils were put together, and laid on cross-beams
connecting the lower ends of the poles as they trail
the ground from the horses' sides, to which they are
attached. Dogs, too, are made useful in this exodus,
and started off, with smaller burdens dragging after
them, in the same manner that horses are packed.

The whole village was in commotion, children
screaming or laughing; dogs barking or growling
under their heavy burdens; squaws running hither

Indian Family on the Move.

The Sun Dance.

and thither, pulling down tipi-poles, packing up
every thing, and leading horses and dogs with huge
burdens.

The small children are placed in sacks of buffalo
skin and hung upon saddles or their mothers' backs.
The wrapped up lodges, which are secured by thongs,
are fastened to the poles on the horses' backs, together
with sundry other articles of domestic use, and upon
these are seated women and children. To guide the
horse a woman goes before, holding the bridle, carrying on her back a load nearly as large as the horse
carries. Women and children are sometimes mounted
upon horses, holding in their arms every variety of
plunder, sometimes little dogs and other forlorn and
hungry looking pets. In this unsightly manner, sometimes two or three thousand families are transported
many miles at the same migration, and, all being in
motion at the same time, the cavalcade extends for a
great distance.

The men and boys are not so unsightly in their appearance, being mounted upon good horses and the
best Indian ponies, riding in groups, leaving the
women and children to trudge along with the burdened horses and dogs.

The number and utility of these faithful dogs is
sometimes astonishing, as they count hundreds, each
bearing a portion of the general household goods.
Two poles, about ten or twelve feet long, are attached

to the shoulders of a dog, leaving one end of each
dragging upon the ground. On these poles a small
burden is carried, and with it the faithful canine jogs
along, looking neither to the right nor to the left, but
apparently intent upon reaching the end of his journey. These faithful creatures are under the charge of
women and children, and their pace is occasionally en-
couraged with admonitions in the form of vigorous
and zealous use of whips applied to their limbs and
sides. It was quite painful to me to see these poor
animals, thus taken from their natural avocation, and
forced to a slavish life of labor, and compelled to
travel along with their burdens; yet, when this change
has been made, they become worthless as hunters, or
watchers, and even for the purpose of barking, being
reduced, instead, to beasts of burden. It was not uncommon to see a great wolfish-looking dog moodily
jogging along with a lot of cooking utensils on one
side, and on the other a crying papoose for a balance,
while his sulking companion toils on, supporting upon
his back a quarter of antelope or elk, and is followed
by an old woman, or some children, who keep at bay
all refractory dogs who run loose, occasionally showing
their superiority by snapping and snarling at their
more unfortunate companions.

This train was immensely large, nearly the whole
Sioux nation having concentrated there for the purpose of war. The chief's sisters brought me a horse

saddled, told me to mount, and accompany the already moving column, that seemed to be spreading far over the hills to the northward. We toiled on all day. Late in the afternoon we arrived at the ground of encampment, and rested for further orders from the warriors, who had gone to battle and would join us there.

I had no means of informing myself at that time with whom the war was raging, but afterward learned that General Sully's army was pursuing the Sioux, and that the engagement was with his men.

In three days the Indians returned to camp, and entered on a course of feasting and rejoicing, that caused me to believe that they had suffered very little loss in the affray.

They passed their day of rest in this sort of entertainment; and here I first saw the scalp dance, which ceremonial did not increase my respect or confidence in the tender mercies of my captors.

This performance is only gone through at night and by the light of torches, consequently its terrible characteristics are heightened by the fantastic gleams of the lighted brands.

The women, too, took part in the dance, and I was forced to mingle in the fearful festivity, painted and dressed for the occasion, and holding a staff from the top of which hung several scalps.

The braves came vauntingly forth, with the most extravagant boasts of their wonderful prowess and courage in war, at the same time brandishing weapons in their hands with the most fearful contortions and threatenings.

A number of young women came with them, carrying the trophies of their friends, which they hold aloft, while the warriors jump around in a circle, brandishing their weapons, and whooping and yelling the fearful war-cry in a most frightful manner, all jumping upon both feet at the same time, with simultaneous stamping and motions with their weapons, keeping exact time. Their gestures impress one as if they were actually cutting and carving each other to pieces as they utter their fearful, sharp yell. They become furious as they grow more excited, until their faces are distorted to the utmost; their glaring eyes protrude with a fiendish, indescribable appearance, while they grind their teeth, and try to imitate the hissing, gurgling sound of death in battle. Furious and faster grows the stamping, until the sight is more like a picture of fiends in a carnival of battle than any thing else to which the war-dance can be compared.

No description can fully convey the terrible sight in all its fearful barbarity, as the bloody trophies of their victory are brandished aloft in the light of the flickering blaze, and their distorted forms were half concealed by darkness. The object for which the scalp is taken is exultation and proof of valor and success. My pen is powerless to portray my feelings during this terrible scene.

This country seemed scarred by countless trails, where the Indian ponies have dragged lodge-poles, in their change of habitations or hunting. The antipathy of the Indian to its occupation or invasion by the wl.ite man is very intense and bitter. The felling of timber, or killing of buffalo, or traveling of a train, or any signs of permanent possession by the white man excites deadly hostility. It is their last hope; if they yield and give up this, they will have to die or ever after be governed by the white man's laws; consequently they lose no opportunity to kill or steal from and harass the whites when they can do so.

The game still clings to its favorite haunts, and the Indian must press upon the steps of the white man or lose all hope of independence. Herds of elk proudly stand with erect antlers, as if charmed by music, or as if curious to understand this strange inroad upon their long-secluded parks of pleasure; the mountain sheep look down from belting crags that skirt the perpendicular northern face of the mountains, and yield no rival of their charms or excellence for food. The black and white-tail deer and antelope are ever present, while the hare and the rabbit, the sage hen, and the prairie-chicken are nearly trodden down before they yield to the intrusion of the stranger.

Brants, wild geese, and ducks multiply and people the waters of beautiful lakes, and are found in many of the streams. The grizzly and cinnamon bears are

often killed and give up their rich material for the
hunter's profit; and the buffalo, in numberless herds,
with tens of thousands in a herd, sweep back and
forth, filling the valley as far as the eye can reach, and
adding their value to the red man both for food, hab-
itation, fuel, and clothing. The Big Horn River,
and mountains and streams beyond, are plentifully
supplied with various kinds of fish. The country
seems to be filled with wolves, which pierce the night
air with their howls, but, like the beavers whose dams
incumber all the smaller streams, and the otter, are
forced to yield their nice coats for the Indian as well
as white man's luxury.

The Indians felt that the proximity of the troops
and their inroads through their best hunting-grounds
would prove disastrous to them and their future hopes
of prosperity, and soon again they were making preparations for battle; and again, on the 8th of August,
the warriors set forth on the war-path, and this time
the action seemed to draw ominously near our encampment.

An Indian boy died the night before, and was buried
rather hastily in the morning. The body was wrapped
in some window curtains that once draped my windows
at Geneva. There was also a red blanket and many
beads and trinkets deposited on an elevated platform,
with the moldering remains, and the bereaved mother
and relatives left the lonely spot with loud lamenta-

tions. There seemed to be great commotion and great anxiety in the movements of the Indians, and presently I could hear the sound of battle; and the echoes, that came back to me from the reports of the guns in the distant hills, warned me of the near approach of my own people, and my heart became a prey to wildly conflicting emotions, as they hurried on in great desperation, and even forbid me turning my head and looking in the direction of the battle. Once I broke the rule and was severely punished for it. They kept their eyes upon me, and were very cross and unkind.

Panting for rescue, yet fearing for its accomplishment, I passed the day. The smoke of action now rose over the hills beyond. The Indians now realized their danger, and hurried on in great consternation.

General Sully's soldiers appeared in close proximity, and I could see them charging on the Indians, who, according to their habits of warfare, skulked behind trees, sending their bullets and arrows vigorously forward into the enemy's ranks. I was kept in advance of the moving column of women and children, who were hurrying on, crying and famishing for water, trying to keep out of the line of firing.

It was late at night before we stopped our pace, when at length we reached the lofty banks of a noble river, but it was some time before they could find a break in the rocky shores which enabled us to reach the water and enjoy the delicious draught, in which luxury the panting horses gladly participated.

We had traveled far and fast all day long, without cessation, through clouds of smoke and dust, parched by a scorching sun. My face was blistered from the burning rays, as I had been compelled to go with my head uncovered, after the fashion of all Indian women. Had not had a drop of water during the whole day.

Reluctant to leave the long-desired acquisition, they all lay down under the tall willows, close to the stream, and slept the sleep of the weary. The horses lingered near, nipping the tender blades of grass that sparsely bordered the stream.

It was not until next morning that I thought of how they should cross the river, which I suppose to have been the Missouri. It was not very wide, but confined between steep banks; it seemed to be deep and quite rapid; they did not risk swimming at that place, to my joy, but went further down and all plunged in and swam across, leading my horse. I was very much frightened, and cried to Heaven for mercy. On that morning we entered a gorge, a perfect mass of huge fragments which had fallen from the mountains above; they led my horse and followed each other closely, and with as much speed as possible, as we were still pursued by the troops. During the day some two or three warriors were brought in wounded. I was called to see them, and assist in dressing their wounds. This being my first experience of the kind, I was at some loss to know what was best to do; but, seeing in it a good opportunity to raise in their estimation, I endeavored to impress them with an air of my superior knowledge of surgery, and as nurse, or medicine woman. I felt now, from their motions and meaning glances, that my life was not safe, since we were so closely pursued over this terrible barren country.

My feelings, all this time, can not be described, when I could hear the sound of the big guns, as the Indians term cannon. I felt that the soldiers had surely come for me and would overtake us, and my heart bounded with joy at the very thought of deliverance, but sunk proportionately when they came to me, bearing their trophies, reeking scalps, soldiers' uniforms, covered with blood, which told its sad story to my aching heart. One day I might be cheered by strong hope of approaching relief, then again would have such assurance of my enemies' success as would sink me correspondingly low in despair. For some reason deception seemed to be their peculiar delight; whether they did it to gratify an insatiable thirst for revenge in themselves, or to keep me more reconciled, more willing and patient to abide, was something I could not determine.

The feelings occasioned by my disappointment in their success can be better imagined than described, but imagination, even in her most extravagant flights, can but poorly picture the horrors that met my view during these running flights.

My constant experience was hope deferred that maketh the heart sick. It was most tantalizing and painful to my spirit to be so near our forces and the flag of liberty, and yet a prisoner and helpless.

On, and still on, we were forced to fly to a place known among them as the Bad Lands, a section of country so wildly desolate and barren as to induce the belief that its present appearance is the effect of volcanic action.

Great bowlders of blasted rock are piled scattering round, and hard, dry sand interspersed among the crevices.

Every thing has a ruined look, as if vegetation and life had formerly existed there, but had been suddenly interrupted by some violent commotion of nature. A terrible blight, like the fulfilling of an ancient curse, darkens the surface of the gloomy landscape, and the desolate, ruinous scene might well represent the entrance to the infernal shades described by classic writers.

A choking wind, with sand, blows continually, and fills the air with dry and blinding dust.

The water is sluggish and dark, and apparently life-destroying in its action, since all that lies around its moistened limits has assumed the form of petrifaction. Rocks though they now seemed, they had formerly held life, both animal and vegetable, and their change will furnish a subject of interesting speculation to enterprising men of science, who penetrate those mournful shades to discover toads, snakes, birds, and a variety of insects, together with plants, trees, and many curiosities, all petrified and having the appearance of stone. I was startled by the strange and wonderful sights.

The terrible scarcity of water and grass urged us forward, and General Sully's army in the rear gave us no rest. The following day or two we were driven so far northward, and became so imminently imperiled by the pursuing forces, that they were obliged to leave all their earthly effects behind them, and swim the Yellow Stone River for life. By this time the ponies were completely famished for want of food and water, so jaded that it was with great difficulty and hard blows that we could urge them on at all.

When Indians are pursued closely, they evince a desperate and reckless desire to save themselves, without regard to property or provisions.

They throw away every thing that will impede flight, and all natural instinct seems lost in fear. We had left, in our compulsory haste, immense quantities of plunder, even lodges standing, which proved immediate help, but in the end a terrible loss.

General Sully with his whole troop stopped to destroy the property, thus giving us an opportunity to escape, which saved us from falling into his hands, as otherwise we inevitably would have done.

One day was consumed in collecting and burning the Indian lodges, blankets, provisions, etc., and that day was used advantageously in getting beyond his reach. They travel constantly in time of war, ranging over vast tracts of country, and prosecuting their battles, or skirmishes, with a quiet determination unknown to the whites.

A few days' pursuit after Indians is generally enough to wear and tire out the ardor of the white man, as it is almost impossible to pursue them through their own country with wagons and supplies for the army, and it is very difficult for American horses to traverse the barren, rugged mountain passes, the Indians having every advantage in their own country, and using their own mode of warfare. The weary soldiers return disheartened by often losing dear comrades, and leaving them in a lonely grave on the plain, dissatisfied with only scattering their red foes.

But the weary savages rest during these intervals, often sending the friendly Indians, as they are called and believed to be, who are received in that character in the forts, and change it for a hostile one, as soon as they reach the hills, to get supplies of ammunition and food with which they refresh themselves and prosecute the war.

After the attack of General Sully was over an Indian came to me with a letter to read, which he had taken from a soldier who was killed by him, and the letter had been found in his pocket. The letter stated that the topographical engineer was killed, and that General Sully's men had caught the red devils and cut their heads off, and stuck them up on poles. The soldier had written a friendly and kind letter to his people, but, ere it was mailed, he was numbered with the dead.

CHAPTER X.

MOURNING FOR THE SLAIN—THREATENED WITH DEATH AT THE FIERY STAKE—SAVED BY A SPEECH FROM OTTAWA—STARVING CONDITION OF THE INDIANS.

As soon as we were safe, and General Sully pursued us no longer, the warriors returned home, and a scene of terrible mourning over the killed ensued among the women. Their cries are terribly wild and distressing, on such occasions; and the near relations of the deceased indulge in frantic expressions of grief that can not be described. Sometimes the practice of cutting the flesh is carried to a horrible and barbarous extent. They inflict gashes on their bodies and limbs an inch in length. Some cut off their hair, blacken their faces, and march through the village in procession, torturing their bodies to add vigor to their lamentations.

Hunger followed on the track of grief; all their food was gone, and there was no game in that portion of the country.

In our flight they scattered every thing, and the country through which we passed for the following two weeks did not yield enough to arrest starvation. The

Indians were terribly enraged, and threatened me with death almost hourly, and in every form.

I had so hoped for liberty when my friends were near; but alas! all my fond hopes were blasted. The Indians told me that the army was going in another direction.

They seemed to have sustained a greater loss than I had been made aware of, which made them feel very revengeful toward me.

The next morning I could see that something unusual was about to happen. Notwithstanding the early hour, the sun scarcely appearing above the horizon, the principal chiefs and warriors were assembled in council, where, judging from the grave and reflective expression of their countenances, they were about to discuss some serious question.

I had reason for apprehension, from their unfriendly manner toward me, and feared for the penalty I might soon have to pay.

Soon they sent an Indian to me, who asked me if I was ready to die—to be burned at the stake. I told him whenever Wakon-Tonka (the Great Spirit) was ready, he would call for me, and then I would be ready and willing to go. He said that he had been sent from the council to warn me, that it had become necessary to put me to death, on account of my white brothers killing so many of their young men recently. He repeated that they were not cruel for the pleasure of being so; necessity is their first law, and he and the wise chiefs, faithful to their hatred for the white race, were in haste to satisfy their thirst for vengeance; and, further, that the interest of their nation required it.

As soon as the chiefs were assembled around the council fire, the pipe-carrier entered the circle, holding in his hand the pipe ready lighted. Bowing to the four cardinal points, he uttered a short prayer, or invocation, and then presented the pipe to the old chief, Ottawa, but retained the bowl in his hand. When all the chiefs and men had smoked, one after the other, the pipe-bearer emptied the ashes into the fire, saying, "Chiefs of the great Dakota nation, Wakon-Tonka give you wisdom, so that whatever be your determination, it may be conformable to justice." Then, after bowing respectfully, he retired.

A moment of silence followed, in which every one seemed to be meditating seriously upon the words that had just been spoken. At length one of the most aged of the chiefs, whose body was furrowed with the scars of innumerable wounds, and who enjoyed among his people a reputation for great wisdom, arose.

Said he, "The pale faces, our eternal persecutors, pursue and harass us without intermission, forcing us to abandon to them, one by one, our best hunting grounds, and we are compelled to seek a refuge in the depths of these Bad Lands, like timid deer. Many of them even dare to come into prairies which belong to us,

to trap beaver, and hunt elk and buffalo, which are
our property. These faithless creatures, the outcasts
of their own people, rob and kill us when they can.
Is it just that we should suffer these wrongs without
complaining? Shall we allow ourselves to be slaughtered like timid Assinneboines, without seking to avenge
ourselves? Does not the law of the Dakotas say,
Justice to our own nation, and death to all pale faces?
Let my brothers say if that is just," pointing to the
stake that was being prepared for me.

"Vengeance is allowable," sententiously remarked
Mahpeah (The Sky).

Another old chief, Ottawa, arose and said, "It is
the undoubted right of the weak and oppressed; and
yet it ought to be proportioned to the injury received. Then why should we put this young, innocent
woman to death? Has she not always been kind to
us, smiled upon us, and sang for us? Do not all our
children love her as a tender sister? Why, then,
should we put her to so cruel a death for the crimes
of others, if they are of her nation? Why should we
punish the innocent for the guilty?"

I looked to Heaven for mercy and protection, offering up those earnest prayers that are never offered in
vain; and oh! how thankful I was when I knew their
decision was to spare my life. Though terrible were
my surroundings, life always became sweet to me,
when I felt that I was about to part with it.

A terrible time ensued, and many dogs, and horses, even, died of starvation. Their bodies were eaten immediately; and the slow but constant march was daily kept up, in hope of game and better facilities for fish and fruit.

Many days in succession I tasted no food, save what I could gather on my way; a few rose leaves and blossoms was all I could find, except the grass I would gather and chew, for nourishment. Fear, fatigue, and long-continued abstinence were wearing heavily on my already shattered frame. Women and children were crying for food; it was a painful sight to witness their sufferings, with no means of alleviating them, and no hope of relief save by traveling and hunting. We had no shelter save the canopy of heaven, and no alternative but to travel on, and at night lie down on the cold, damp ground, for a resting place.

If I could but present to my readers a truthful picture of that Indian home at that time, with all its sorrowful accompaniments! They are certainly engraved upon faithful memory, to last forever; but no touch of pen could give any semblance of the realities to another.

What exhibitions of their pride and passion I have seen; what ideas of their intelligence and humanity I have been compelled to form; what manifestations of their power and ability to govern had been thrust upon me. The treatment received was not such as to enhance in any wise a woman's admiration for the so-called noble red man, but rather to make one pray to be delivered from their power.

Compelled to travel many days in succession, and to experience the gnawings of hunger without mitigation, every day had its share of toil and fear. Yet while my temporal wants were thus poorly supplied, I was not wholly denied spiritual food. It was a blessed consolation that no earthly foe could interrupt my communion with the heavenly world. In my midnight, wakeful hours, I was visited with many bright visions.

> He walks with thee, that angel kind,
> And gently whispers, be resigned;
> Bear up, bear on, the end shall tell,
> The dear Lord ordereth all things well.

CHAPTER XI.

MEET ANOTHER WHITE FEMALE CAPTIVE—SAD STORY OF MARY BOYEAU
—A CHILD ROASTED AND ITS BRAINS DASHED OUT—MURDER OF
MRS. FLETCHER—FIVE CHILDREN SLAUGHTERED—FATE OF THEIR
MOTHER.

IT was about this time that I had the sorrowful satisfaction of meeting with a victim of Indian cruelty,
whose fate was even sadder than mine.

It was a part of my labor to carry water from the
stream at which we camped, and, awakened for that
purpose, I arose and hurried out one morning before
the day had yet dawned clearly, leaving the Indians
still in their blankets, and the village very quiet.

In the woods beyond I heard the retiring howl of
the wolf, the shrill shriek of the bird of prey, as it
was sweeping down on the unburied carcass of some
poor, murdered traveler, and the desolation of my life
and its surroundings filled my heart with dread and
gloom.

I was so reduced in strength and spirit, that nothing
but the dread of the scalping-knife urged my feet from
task to task; and now, returning toward the tipi,
with my heavy bucket, I was startled to behold a fair-

faced, beautiful young girl sitting there, dejected and worn, like myself, but bearing the marks of loveliness and refinement, despite her neglected covering.

Almost doubting my reason, for I had become unsettled in my self-reliance, and even sanity, I feared to address her, but stood spell-bound, gazing in her sad brown eyes and drooping, pallid face.

The chief stood near the entrance of the tipi, enjoying the cool morning air, and watching the interview with amusement. He offered me a book, which chanced to be one of the Willson's readers, stolen from our wagons, and bade me show it to the stranger.

I approached the girl, who instantly held out her hand, and said: " What book is that? "

The sound of my own language, spoken by one of my own people, was too much for me, and I sank to the ground by the side of the stranger, and, endeavoring to clasp her in my arms, became insensible.

A kindly squaw, who was in sight, must have been touched by our helpless sorrow; for, when recovering, she was sprinkling my face with water from the bucket, and regarding me with looks of interest.

Of course, we realized that this chance interview would be short, and, perhaps, the last that we would be able to enjoy, and, while my companion covered her face and wept, I told my name and the main incidents of my capture; and I dreaded to recall the possible fate of my Mary, lest I should rouse the terrible feelings I was trying to keep in subjection as my only hope of preserving reason.

The young girl responded to my confidence by giving her own story, which she related to me as follows:

"My name is Mary Boyeau; these people call me Madee. I have been among them since the massacre in Minnesota, and am now in my sixteenth year. My parents were of French descent, but we lived in the State of New York, until my father, in pursuance of his peculiar passion for the life of a naturalist and a man of science, sold our eastern home, and came to live on the shores of Spirit Lake, Minnesota.

"The Indians had watched about our place, and regarded what they had seen of my father's chemical apparatus with awe and fear. Perhaps they suspected him of working evil charms in his laboratory, or held his magnets, microscopes, and curiously-shaped tubes in superstitious aversion.

"I can not tell; I only know that we were among the first victims of the massacre, and that all my family were murdered except myself, and, I fear, one younger sister."

"You fear!" said I. "Do you not hope that she escaped?"

The poor girl shook her head. "From a life like mine death is an escape," she said, bitterly.

"Oh! it is fearful! and a sin to rush unbidden into God's presence, but I can not live through another frightful winter.

"No, I must and will die if no relief comes to me. For a year these people regarded me as a child, and then a young man of their tribe gave a horse for me, and carried me to his tipi as his wife."

"Do you love your husband?" I asked.

A look, bitter and revengeful, gleamed from her eyes.

"Love a savage, who bought me to be a drudge and slave!" she repeated. "No! I hate him as I hate all that belong to this fearful bondage. He has another wife and a child. Thank God!" she added, with a shudder, "that I am not a mother!"

Misery and the consciousness of her own degraded life seemed to have made this poor young creature desperate; and, looking at her toil-worn hands and scarred arms, I saw the signs of abuse and cruelty; her feet, too, were bare, and fearfully bruised and travel-marked.

"Does he ill treat you?" I inquired.

"His wife does," she answered. "I am forced to do all manner of slavish work, and when my strength fails, I am urged on by blows. Oh! I do so fearfully dread the chilling winters, without proper food or clothing; and I long to lie down and die, if God's mercy will only permit me to escape from this hopeless imprisonment. I have nothing to expect now. I did once look forward to release, but that is all gone. I strove to go with the others, who were ransomed at Fort Pierre, and Mrs. Wright plead for me with all her heart; but the man who bought me would not give me up, and my prayers were useless.

" Mr. Dupuy, a Frenchman, who brought a wagon for the redeemed women and children, did not offer enough for me; and when another man offered a horse my captor would not receive it.

" There were many prisoners that I did not see in the village, but I am left alone. The Yanktons, who hold me, are friendly by pretense, and go to the agencies for supplies and annuities, but at heart they are bitterly hostile. They assert that, if they did not murder and steal, the Father at Washington would forget them; and now they receive presents and supplies to keep them in check, which they delight in taking, and deceiving the officers as to their share in the outbreaks."

Her dread of soldiers was such that she had never attempted to escape, nor did she seem to think it possible to get away from her present life, so deep was the despair into which long-continued suffering had plunged her.

Sad as my condition was, I could not but pity poor Mary's worse fate. The unwilling wife of a brutal savage, and subject to all the petty malice of a scarcely less brutal squaw, there could be no gleam of sunshine in her future prospects. True, I was, like her, a captive, torn from home and friends, and subject to harsh treatment, but no such personal indignity had fallen to my lot.

When Mary was first taken, she saw many terrible things, which she related to me, among which was the following:

One day, the Indians went into a house where they found a woman making bread. Her infant child lay in the cradle, unconscious of its fate. Snatching it from its little bed they thrust it into the heated oven, its screams torturing the wretched mother, who was immediately after stabbed and cut in many pieces.

Taking the suffering little creature from the oven, they then dashed out its brains against the walls of the house.

One day, on their journey, they came to a narrow but deep stream of water. Some of the prisoners, and nearly all of the Indians, crossed on horseback, while a few crossed on logs, which had been cut down by the beaver. A lady (by name Mrs. Fletcher, I believe), who was in delicate health, fell into the water with her heavy burden, unable, on account of her condition, to cross, and was shot by the Indians, her lifeless body soon disappearing from sight. She also told me of a white man having been killed a few days previous, and a large sum of money taken from him, which would be exchanged for articles used among the Indians when they next visited the Red River or British Possessions. They went, she told me, two or three times a year, taking American horses, valuables, etc., which they had stolen from the whites, and exchanging them for amunition, powder, arrow points, and provisions.

Before they reached the Missouri River they killed five of Mrs. Dooley's children, one of which was left on the ground in a place where the distracted mother had to pass daily in carrying water from the river; and when they left the camp the body remained unburied. So terrible were the sufferings of this heartbroken mother, that, when she arrived in safety among the whites, her reason was dethroned, and I was told that she was sent to the lunatic asylum, where her distracted husband soon followed.

Mary wished that we might be together, but knew that it would be useless to ask, as it would not be granted.

I gave her my little book and half of my pencil, which she was glad to receive. I wrote her name in the book, together with mine, encouraging her with every kind word and hope of the future. She could read and write, and understood the Indian language thoroughly.

The book had been taken from our wagon, and I had endeavored to teach the Indians from it, for it contained several stories; so it made the Indians very angry to have me part with it.

For hours I had sat with the book in my hands, showing them the pictures and explaining their meaning, which interested them greatly, and which helped pass away and relieve the monotony of the days of captivity which I was enduring. Moreover, it inspired them with a degree of respect and veneration for me when engaged in the task, which was not only pleasant, but a great comfort. It was by this means they discovered my usefulness in writing letters and reading for them.

I found them apt pupils, willing to learn, and they learned easily and rapidly. Their memory is very retentive—unusually good.

CHAPTER XII.

FIRST INTIMATION OF MY LITTLE MARY'S FATE—DESPAIR AND DELI-
RIUM—A SHOWER OF GRASSHOPPERS—A FEAST AND A FIGHT—
AN ENRAGED SQUAW—THE CHIEF WOUNDED.

ONE day, as I was pursuing what seemed to me an
endless journey, an Indian rode up beside me, whom I
did not remember to have seen before.

At his saddle hung a bright and well-known little
shawl, and from the other side was suspended a child's
scalp of long, fair hair.

As my eyes rested on the frightful sight, I trembled
in my saddle and grasped the air for support. A
blood-red cloud seemed to come between me and the
outer world, and I realized that innocent victim's dying
agonies.

The torture was too great to be endured—a merciful
insensibility interposed between me and madness.

I dropped from the saddle as if dead, and rolled upon
the ground at the horse's feet.

When I recovered, I was clinging to a squaw, who,
with looks of astonishment and alarm, was vainly
endeavoring to extricate herself from my clutches.

With returning consciousness, I raised my eyes to the fearful sight that had almost deprived me of reason; it was gone.

The Indian had suspected the cause of my emotion, and removed it out of sight.

They placed me in the saddle once more, and not being able to control the horrible misery I felt, I protested wildly against their touch, imploring them to kill me, and frantically inviting the death I had before feared and avoided.

When they camped, I had not the power or reason to seek my own tent, but fell down in the sun, where the chief found me lying. He had been out at the head of a scouting party, and knew nothing of my sufferings.

Instantly approaching me, he inquired who had misused me. I replied, "No one. I want to see my dear mother, my poor mother, who loves me, and pines for her unhappy child."

I had found, by experience, that the only grief with which this red nation had any sympathy was the sorrow one might feel for a separation from a mother, and even the chief seemed to recognize the propriety of such emotion.

On this account I feigned to be grieving solely for my dear widowed mother, and was treated with more consideration than I had dared to expect.

Leaving me for a few moments, he returned, bringing me some ripe wild plums, which were deliciously cooling to my fever-parched lips.

Hunger and thirst, sorrow and fear, with unusual fatigue and labor, had weakened me in mind and body, so that, after trying to realize the frightful vision that had almost deprived me of my senses, I began to waver in my knowledge of it, and half determined that it was a hideous phantom, like many another that had tortured my lonely hours.

I tried to dismiss the awful dream from remembrance, particularly as the days that followed found me ill and delirious, and it was some time before I was able to recall events clearly.

About this time there was another battle; and many having already sank under the united misery of hunger and fatigue, the camp was gloomy and hopeless in the extreme.

The Indians discovered my skill in dressing wounds, and I was called immediately to the relief of the wounded brought into camp.

The fight had lasted three days, and, from the immoderate lamentations, I supposed many had fallen, but could form no idea of the loss.

Except when encamped for rest, the tribe pursued their wanderings constantly; sometimes flying before the enemy, at others endeavoring to elude them.

I kept the record of time, as it passed with the savages, as well as I was able, and, with the exception of a few days lost, during temporary delirium and fever at two separate times, and which I endeavored to supply by careful inquiry, I missed no count of the rising or setting sun, and knew dates almost as well as if I had been in the heart of civilization.

One very hot day, a dark cloud seemed suddenly to pass before the sun and threaten a great storm. The wind rose, and the cloud became still darker, until the light of day was almost obscured.

A few drops sprinkled the earth, and, then, in a heavy, blinding, and apparently inexhaustible shower, fell a countless swarm of grasshoppers, covering every thing and rendering the air almost black by their descent.

It is impossible to convey an idea of their extent; they seemed to rival Pharaoh's locusts in number, and no doubt would have done damage to the food of the savages had they not fallen victims themselves to their keen appetites.

To catch them, large holes are dug in the ground, which are heated by fires. Into these apertures the insects are then driven, and, the fires having been removed, the heated earth bakes them.

They are considered good food, and were greedily devoured by the famishing Sioux. Although the grasshoppers only remained two days, and went as suddenly as they had come, the Indians seemed refreshed by feasting on such small game, and continued to move forward.

Halting one day to rest beside good water, I busily engaged myself in the chief's tipi, or lodge. I had grown so weak that motion of any kind was exhausting to me, and I could scarcely walk. I felt that I must soon die of starvation and sorrow, and life had ceased to be dear to me.

Mechanically I tried to fulfill my tasks, so as to secure the continued protection of the old squaw, who, when not incensed by passion, was not devoid of kindness.

My strength failed me, and I could not carry out my wishes, and almost fell as I tried to move around.

This met with disapprobation, and, better fed than myself, she could not sympathize with my want of strength. She became cross, and left the lodge, threatening me with her vengeance.

Presently an Indian woman, who pitied me, ran into the tipi in great haste, saying that her husband had got some deer meat, and she had cooked it for a feast, and begged me to share it. As she spoke, she drew me toward her tent, and, hungry and fainting, I readily followed.

The chief saw us go, and, not disdaining a good dinner, he followed. The old squaw came flying into the lodge like an enraged fury, flourishing her knife, and vowing she would kill me.

I arose immediately and fled, the squaw pursuing me. The chief attempted to interfere, but her rage was too great, and he struck her, at which she sprang like an infuriated tiger upon him, stabbing him in several places.

Her brother, who at a short distance beheld the fray, and deeming me the cause, fired six shots, determining to kill me. One of these shots lodged in the arm of the chief, breaking it near the shoulder. I then ran until I reached the outskirts of the village, where I was captured by a party who saw me running, but who knew not the cause.

Thinking that I was endeavoring to escape, they dragged me in the tent, brandishing their tomahawks and threatening vengeance.

After the lapse of half an hour some squaws came and took me back to the lodge of the chief, who was waiting for me, before his wounds could be dressed. He was very weak from loss of blood.

I never saw the wife of the chief afterward.

Indian surgery is coarse and rude in its details. A doctor of the tribe had pierced the arm of the chief with a long knife, probing in search of the ball it had received, and the wound thus enlarged had to be healed.

As soon as I was able to stand, I was required to go and wait on the disabled chief. I found his three sisters with him, and with these I continued to live in companionship.

One of them had been married, at the fort, to a white man, whom she had left at Larimie when his prior wife arrived.

She told me that they were esteemed friendly, and had often received supplies from the fort, although at heart they were always the enemy of the white man.

"But will they not suspect you?" asked I. "They may discover your deceit and punish you some day."

She laughed derisively. "Our prisoners don't escape to tell tales," she replied. "Dead people don't talk. We claim friendship, and they can not prove that we don't feel it. Besides, all white soldiers are cowards."

Shudderingly I turned away from this enemy of my race, and prepared to wait on my captor, whose superstitious belief in the healing power of a white woman's touch led him to desire her services.

The wounds of the chief were severe, and the suppuration profuse. It was my task to bathe and dress them, and prepare his food.

Hunting and fishing being now out of the question for him, he had sent his wives to work for themselves, keeping the sisters and myself to attend him.

War with our soldiers seemed to have decreased the power of the chief to a great extent.

As he lay ill, he evidently meditated on some plan of strengthening his forces, and finally concluded to send an offer of marriage to the daughter of a war-chief of another band.

As General Sully's destructive attack had deprived him all ready offerings, he availed himself of my shoes, which happened to be particularly good, and, reducing me to moccasins, sent them as a gift to the expected bride.

She evidently received them graciously, for she came to his lodge almost every day to visit him, and sat chatting at his side, to his apparent satisfaction.

The pleasure of this new matrimonial acquisition on the part of the chief was very trying to me, on account of my limited wardrobe, for as the betrothed continued in favor, the chief evinced it by giving her articles of my clothing.

An Indian woman had given me a red silk sash, such as officers wear. The chief unceremoniously cut it in half, leaving me one half, while the coquettish squaw received the rest.

An Indian husband's power is absolute, even to death.

No woman can have more than one husband, but an Indian can have as many wives as he chooses.

The marriage of the chief was to be celebrated with all due ceremony when his arm got well.

But his arm never recovered. Mr. Clemens, the interpreter, tells me (in my late interview with him), that he still remains crippled, and unable to carry out his murderous intentions, or any of his anticipated wicked designs.

He is now living in the forts along the Missouri River, gladly claiming support from the Government.

CHAPTER XIII.

ARRIVAL OF "PORCUPINE"—A LETTER FROM CAPTAIN MARSHALL—
HOPES OF RESCUE—TREACHERY OF THE MESSENGER—EGOSEGALO-
NICHA—THE TABLES TURNED—ANOTHER GLEAM OF HOPE—THE
INDIAN "WHITE TIPI"—DISAPPOINTED—A WHITE MAN BOUND
AND LEFT TO STARVE—A BURIAL INCIDENT.

BEFORE the Indians left this camping-ground, there
arrived among us an Indian called Porcupine. He
was well dressed, and mounted on a fine horse, and
brought with him presents and valuables that insured
him a cordial reception.

After he had been a few days in the village, he
gave me a letter from Captain Marshall, of the Eleventh Ohio Cavalry, detailing the unsuccessful attempts
that had been made to rescue me, and stating that this
friendly Indian had undertaken to bring me back, for
which he would be rewarded.

The letter further said that he had already received
a horse and necessary provisions for the journey, and
had left his three wives, with thirteen others, at the
fort, as hostages.

My feelings, on reading this letter, were indescribable. My heart leaped with unaccustomed hope, at this evidence of the efforts of my white friends in my behalf; but the next instant despair succeeded this gleam of happy anticipation, for I knew this faithless messenger would not be true to his promise, since he had joined the Sioux immediately after his arrival among them, in a battle against the whites.

My fears were not unfounded. Porcupine prepared to go back to the fort without me, disregarding my earnest prayers and entreaties.

The chief found me useful, and determined to keep me. He believed that a woman who had seen so much of their deceitfulness and cruelty could do them injury at the fort, and might prevent their receiving annuities.

Porcupine said he should report me as dead, or impossible to find; nor could I prevail on him to do any thing to the contrary.

When reminded of the possible vengeance of the soldiers on his wives, whom they had threatened to kill if he did not bring me back, he laughed.

"The white soldiers are cowards," he replied; "they never kill women; and I will deceive them as I have done before."

Saying this, he took his departure; nor could my most urgent entreaties induce the chief to yield his consent, and allow me to send a written message to my friends, or in any wise assure them of my existence.

All hope of rescue departed, and sadly I turned again to the wearisome drudgery of my captive life.

The young betrothed bride of the old chief was very gracious to me. On one occasion she invited me to join her in a walk. The day was cool, and the air temptingly balmy.

"Down there," she said, pointing to a deep ravine; "come and walk there; it is cool and shady."

I looked in the direction indicated, and then at the Indian girl, who became very mysterious in her manner, as she whispered:

"There are white people down there."

"How far?" I asked, eagerly.

"About fifty miles," she replied. "They have great guns, and men dressed in much buttons; their wagons are drawn by horses with long ears."

A fort, thought I, but remembering the treacherous nature of the people I was among, I repressed every sign of emotion, and tried to look indifferent.

"Should you like to see them?" questioned Egose-galonicha, as she was called.

"They are strangers to me," I said, quietly; "I do not know them."

"Are you sorry to live with us?"

"You do not have such bread as I would like to eat," replied I, cautiously.

"And are you dissatisfied with our home?"

"You have some meat now; it is better than that at

the other camping-ground. There we had no food, and I suffered."

"But your eyes are swollen and red," hinted she; "you do not weep for bread."

These questions made me suspicious, and I tried to evade the young squaw, but in vain.

"Just see how green that wood is," I said, affecting not to hear her.

"But you do not say you are content," repeated she. "Will you stay here always, willingly?"

"Come and listen to the birds," said I, drawing my companion toward the grove.

I did not trust her, and feared to utter a single word, lest it might be used against me with the chief.

Neither was I mistaken in the design of Egosegalo-nicha, for when we returned to the lodge, I overheard her relating to the chief the amusement she had enjoyed, in lying to the white woman, repeating what she had said about the fort, and inventing entreaties which I had used, urging her to allow me to fly to my white friends, and leave the Indians forever.

Instantly I resolved to take advantage of the affair as a joke, and, approaching the chief with respectful pleasantry, begged to reverse the story.

It was the squaw who had implored me to go with her to the white man's fort, I said, and find her a white warrior for a husband; but, true to my faith with the Indians, I refused.

The wily Egosegalonicha, thus finding her weapons turned against herself, appeared confused, and suddenly left the tent, at which the old chief smiled grimly.

Slander, like a vile serpent, coils itself among these Indian women; and, as with our fair sisters in civilized society, when reality fails, invention is called in to suply the defect. They delight in scandal, and prove by it their claim to some of the refined conventionalities of civilized life.

Porcupine had spread the news abroad in the village that a large reward had been offered for the white woman, consequently I was sought for, the motive being to gain the reward.

One day an Indian, whom I had seen in different places, and whose wife I had known, made signs intimating a desire for my escape, and assuring me of his help to return to my people.

I listened to his plans, and although I knew my position in such a case to be one of great peril, yet I felt continually that my life was of so little value that any opportunity, however slight, was as a star in the distance, and escape should be attempted, even at a risk.

We conversed as well as we could several times, and finally arrangements were made. At night he was to make a slight scratching noise at the tipi where I was, as a sign. The night came, but I was singing to the people, and could not get away. Another time we had visitors in the lodge, and I would be missed. The next night I arose from my robe, and went out into the darkness. Seeing my intended rescuer at a short distance, I approached and followed him. We ran hastily out of the village about a mile, where we were to be joined by the squaw who had helped make the arrangements and was favorable to the plan for my escape, but she was not there. White Tipi (that was the Indian's name) looked hastily around, and, seeing no one, darted suddenly away, without a word of explanation. Why the Indian acted thus I never knew. It was a strange proceeding.

Fear lent me wings, and I flew, rather than ran, back to my tipi, or lodge, where, exhausted and discouraged, I dropped on the ground and feigned slumber, for the inmates were already aroused, having just discovered my absence. Finding me apparently asleep, they lifted me up, and taking me into the tent, laid me upon my own robe.

The next evening White Tipi sent for me to come to his lodge, to a feast, where I was well and hospitably entertained, but not a sign given of the adventure of the previous night. But when the pipe was passed, he requested it to be touched to my lips, then offered it to the Great Spirit, thus signifying his friendship for me.

In this month the Indians captured a white man, who was hunting on the prairie, and carried him far away from the haunts of white men, where they tied him hand and foot, after divesting him of all clothing, and left him to starve. He was never heard of afterward.

There were twin children in one of the lodges, one of which sickened and died, and in the evening was buried. The surviving child was placed upon the scaffold by the corpse, and there remained all night, its crying and moaning almost breaking my heart. I inquired why they did this. The reply was, to cause the mate to mourn. The mother was on one of the neighboring hills, wailing and weeping, as is the custom among them. Every night, nearly, there were women among the hills, wailing for their dead.

CHAPTER XIV.

LOST IN THE INDIAN VILLAGE—BLACK BEAR'S WHITE WIFE—A SMALL
TEA PARTY—THE WHITE BOY-CAPTIVE, CHARLES SYLVESTER—
THE SUN DANCE—A CONCILIATING LETTER FROM GENERAL SIB-
LEY—A PUZZLE OF HUMAN BONES—THE INDIAN AS AN ARTIST—
I DESTROY A PICTURE AND AM PUNISHED WITH FIRE-BRANDS—A
SICK INDIAN.

ABOUT the 1st of October the Indians were on the
move as usual, and by some means I became separated
from the family I was with, and was lost. I looked
around for them, but their familiar faces were not to be
seen. Strangers gazed upon me, and, although I besought them to assist me in finding the people of my
own tipi, they paid no attention to my trouble, and
refused to do any thing for me.

Never shall I forget the sadness I felt as evening
approached, and we encamped for the night in a lonely
valley, after a wearisome day's journey.

Along one side stood a strip of timber, with a small
stream beside it. Hungry, weary, and lost to my
people, with no place to lay my head, and after a fruit-
less search for the family, I was more desolate than
ever. Even Keoku, or "Yellow Bird," the Indian

girl who had been given me, was not with me that day, making it still more lonely.

I sat down and held my pony. It was autumn, and the forest wore the last glory of its gorgeous coloring. Already the leaves lay along the paths, like a rich carpet of variegated colors. The winds caught a deeper tone, mournful as the tones of an Æolian harp, but the air was balmy and soft, and the sunlight lay warm and pleasant, as in midsummer, over the beautiful valley, now occupied with numberless camps of tentless Indians. It seemed as if the soft autumn weather was, to the last moment, unwilling to yield the last traces of beauty to the chill embraces of stern winter, and I thought of the luxuries and comforts of my home. I looked back on the past with tears of sorrow and regret; my heart was overburdened with grief, and I prayed to die. The future looked like a dark cloud approaching, for the dread of the desolation of winter to me was appalling.

While meditating on days of the past, and contemplating the future, Keoku came suddenly upon me, and was delighted to find the object of her search.

They had been looking for me, and did not know where I had gone, were quite worried about me, she said, and she was glad she had found me. I was as pleased as herself, and rejoiced to join them.

One has no idea of the extent of an Indian village, or of the number of its inhabitants.

It would seem strange to some that I should ever get lost when among them, but, like a large city, one may be separated from their companions, and in a few moments be lost.

The Indians all knew the "white woman," but I knew but few comparatively, and consequently when among strangers I felt utterly friendless.

The experience of those days of gloom and sadness seem like a fearful dream, now that my life is once again with civilized people, and enjoying the blessings that I was there deprived of.

Some twenty-five years ago an emigrant train, en route for California, arrived in the neighborhood of the crossing of the North Platte, and the cholera broke out among the travelers, and every one died, with the exception of one little girl.

The Indian "Black Bear," while hunting, came to the wagons, now a morgue, and, finding the father of the girl dying with cholera, took the child in his arms. The dying parent begged him to carry his little one to his home in the East, assuring him of abundant reward by the child's friends, in addition to the gold he gave him. These facts I gleaned from a letter given to Black Bear by the dying father, and which had been carefully preserved by the daughter.

Instead of doing as was desired, he took the money, child, and every thing valuable in the train, to his own home among the hills, and there educated the little one with habits of savage life.

She forgot her own language, her name, and every thing about her past life, but she knew that she was white. Her infancy and girlhood were, therefore, passed in utter ignorance of the modes of life of her own people, and, contented and happy, she remained among them, verifying the old adage, that "habit is second nature." When she was of marriageable age, Black Bear took her for his wife, and they had a child, a boy.

I became acquainted with this white woman shortly after I went into the village, and we were sincere friends, although no confidants, as I dared not trust her. It was very natural and pleasant also to know her, as she was white, and although she was an Indian in tastes and habits, she was my sister, and belonged to my people; there was a sympathetic chord between us, and it was a relief to be with her.

On the occasion of my first visit with her, Black Bear suggested the idea that white women always drank tea together, so she made us a cup of herb tea, which we drank in company.

I endeavored to enlighten her, and to do her all the good I could; told her of the white people, and of their kindness and Christianity, trying to impress her with the superiority of the white race, all of which she listened to with great interest.

I was the only white woman she had seen, for whenever they neared any fort she was always kept out of sight.

She seemed to enjoy painting herself, and dressing for the dances, as well as the squaws, and was happy and contented with Indian surroundings, for she knew no difference.

I know not what has become of her, for I have never heard; neither can I remember the name of her father, which was in the note handed the Indian by his dying hand.

A little boy, fourteen years old, whose name was Charles Sylvester, belonging in Quincy, Illinois, who was stolen when seven years of age, was in the village, and one day I saw him playing with the Indian boys, and, discovering immediately that he was a white boy, I flew to his side, and tried to clasp him in my arms, in my joy exclaiming, "Oh! I know you are a white boy! Speak to me, and tell me who you are and where you come from?" He also had forgotten his name and parentage, but knew that he was white.

When I spoke to him, the boys began to plague and tease him, and he refused to speak to me, running away every time I approached him.

One year after, one day, when this boy was out hunting, he killed a comrade by accident, and he dared not return to the village; so he escaped, on his pony, to the white people. On his way to the States, he called at a house where they knew what Indians he belonged to, and they questioned him, whether he had seen a white woman in the village; he replied in the affirmative, and a bundle of pictures being given him, he picked mine out from among them, saying, "That is the white woman whom I saw."

After a while, being discontented with his own people, he returned to his adopted friends on the North Platte, and became an interpreter and trader, and still remains there, doing business at various posts.

When the Indians went to obtain their annuities, they transferred me to the Unkpapas, leaving me in their charge, where there was a young couple, and an old Indian, who had four wives; he had been very brave, it was said, for he had endured the trial which proves the successful warrior. He was one of those who "looked at the sun" without failing in heart or strength.

This custom is as follows: The one who undergoes this operation is nearly naked, and is suspended from the upper end of a pole by a cord, which is tied to some splints which run through the flesh of both breasts. The weight of his body is hung from it, the feet still upon the ground helping support it a very little, and in his left hand he holds his favorite bow, and in his right, with a firm hold, his medicine bag.

A great crowd usually looks on, sympathizing with and encouraging him, but he still continues to hang and "look at the sun," without paying the least attention to any one about him. The mystery men beat their drums, and shake their rattles, and sing as loud as they can yell, to strengthen his heart to look at the sun from its rising until its setting, at which time, if his heart and strength have not failed him, he is "cut down," receives a liberal donation of presents, which are piled before him during the day, and also the name and style of a doctor, or medicine man, which lasts him, and insures him respect, through life. It is considered a test of bravery. Superstition seems to have full sway among the Indians—just as much as in heathen lands beyond the sea, where the Burmah mother casts her child to the crocodile to appease the Great Spirit.

Many of these Indians were from Minnesota, and were of the number that escaped justice two years before, after committing an indiscriminate slaughter of men, women, and children. One day, I was sent for by one of them, and when I was seated in his lodge, he gave me a letter to read, which purported to have been written by General Sibley, as follows:

"This Indian, after taking part in the present outbreak of the Indians against the white settlers and missionaries, being sick, and not able to keep up with his friends in their flight, we give you the offerings of friendship, food and clothing. You are in our power, but we won't harm you. Go to your people and gladden their hearts. Lay down your weapons, and fight the white men no more. We will do you good, and not evil. Take this letter; in it we have spoken. Depart in peace, and ever more be a friend to the white people, and you will be more happy.

H. H. SIBLEY,
Brig · Gen., Commanding Expedition.

Insfinctively I looked up into his face, and said: "Intend to keep your promise?" He laughed derisively at the idea of an Indian brave abandoning his profession. He told of many instances of outrageous cruelties of his band in their marauding and murderous attacks on traveling parties and frontier settlers; and, further, to assure me of his bravery, he showed me a puzzle or game he had made from the finger bones of some of the victims that had fallen beneath his own tomahawk. The bones had been freed from the flesh by boiling, and, being placed upon a string, were used for playing some kind of Indian game. This is but one of the heathenish acts of these Indians.

The Indians are fond of recounting their exploits, and, savage like, dwell with much satisfaction upon the number of scalps they have taken from their white foes. They would be greatly amused at the shuddering horror manifested, when, to annoy me, they would tauntingly portray the dying agonies of white men, women, and children, who had fallen into their hands;

and especially would the effect of their description **of** the murder of little Mary afford them satisfaction. I feel, now, that I must have been convinced of her death, yet I could not then help hoping that she had escaped.

These exploits and incidents are generally related by the Indians, when in camp having nothing to do. The great lazy brutes would sit by the hour, making carricatures of white soldiers, representing them in various ways, and always as cowards and inferior beings; sometimes as in combat, but always at their mercy. This was frequently done, apparently to annoy me, and one day, losing patience, I snatched a rude drawing from the hands of an Indian, who was holding it up to my view, and tore it in two, clasping the part that represented the white soldier to my heart, and throwing the other in the fire. Then, looking up, I told them the white soldiers were dear to me; that they were my friends, and I loved them. I said they were friends to the Indians, and did not want to harm them. I expressed myself in the strongest manner by words and signs.

Never did I see a more enraged set of men. They assailed me with burning fire-brands, burning me severely. They heated the points of arrows, and burned and threatened me sorely.

I told them I meant no harm to them. That it was ridiculous, their getting angry at my burning a bit of paper. I promised I would make them some more; that they should have pictures of my drawing, when, at last, I pacified them. They were much like children in this respect—easily offended, but very difficult to please.

I was constantly annoyed, worried, and terrified by their strange conduct—their transition from laughing and fun to anger, and even rage. I knew not how to get along with them. One moment, they would seem friendly and kind; the next, if any act of mine displeased them, their faces were instantly changed, and they displayed their hatred or anger in unmeasured words or conduct—children one hour, the next, fiends. I always tried to please them, and was as cheerful as I could be under the circumstances, for my own sake.

One day, I was called to see a man who lay in his tipi in great suffering. His wasted face was darkened by fever, and his brilliantly restless eyes rolled anxiously, as if in search of relief from pain. He was reduced to a skeleton, and had endured tortures from the suppuration of an old wound in the knee.

He greeted me with the "How! how!" of Indian politeness, and, in answer to my inquiry why he came to suffer so, replied:

"I go to fight white man. He take away land, and chase game away; then he take away our squaws. He take away my best squaw."

Here his voice choked, and he displayed much emotion.

Pitying his misery, I endeavored to aid him, and rendered him all the assistance in my power, but death was then upon him.

The medicine man was with him also, practicing his incantations.

We were so constantly traveling, it wearied me beyond expression. The day after the Indian's burial we were again on the move.

CHAPTER XV.

PREPARING THE OHI-OHA-OHA, OR KILLIKINNICK—ATTACK ON CAP-
TAIN FISK'S EMIGRANT TRAIN — FOURTEEN WHITES KILLED —
A BIG HAUL OF WHISKY—A DRUNKEN DEBAUCH—I WRITE A
LETTER TO CAPTAIN FISK UNDER DICTATION—POISONED INDIANS—
THE TRAIN SAVED BY MY CLERICAL STRATEGY.

ONE of the occupations given me, while resting in
the villages between war times, was to prepare the
bark of a red willow called killikinnick, for smoking
instead of tobacco.

They discovered that I could sing, and groups of
idle warriors would gather around me before the tent,
urging me to sing as I worked. A dreary, dreary
task! chanting to please my savage companions while
I rubbed and prepared the bark of willow, my heart
ready to burst with grief.

On the 5th of September they went to battle, and
surprised a portion of Captain Fisk's men passing in
escorting an emigrant train—fourteen of whom they
killed, and captured two wagons loaded with whisky,
wines, and valuable articles. There was a quantity of
silver-ware and stationery also taken by them.

Among the articles captured and brought into camp

were a number of pickles in glass jars, which the Indians tasted. The result was comical in the extreme, for there is nothing that an Indian abhors more than a strong acid. The faces they made can be imagined but not described. Thinking they might be improved by cooking, they placed the jars in the fire, when of course they exploded, very much to their disgust for the "white man's kettles."

I could hear the firing plainly, and when they returned that night in triumph, bringing with them the plundered stores, they committed every description of extravagant demonstration. In the wild orgies which followed, they mocked and groaned in imitation of the dying, and went through a horrid mimicry of the butchery they had perpetrated.

They determined to go out again, and capture a quantity of horses corralled in the neighborhood, and sweep the train and soldiers with wholesale massacre; but they feared the white man's cannon, and deliberated on means of surprising by ambush, which is their only idea of warfare.

Indians are not truly brave, though they are vain of the name of courage. Cunning, stealth, strategy, and deceit are the weapons they use in attack.

They endure pain, because they are taught from infancy that it is cowardly to flinch, but they will never stand to fight if they can strike secretly and escape.

Fearing the cannon, yet impatient for the spoil

almost within view, the Indians waited for three days for the train to move on and leave them free to attack.

For two days I implored and begged on my knees to be allowed to go with them, but to no avail. At last I succeeded in inducing them to allow me to write, as they knew I understood the nature of correspondence, and they procured for me the necessary appliances and dictated a letter to Captain Fisk, assuring him that the Indians were weary of fighting, and advising him to go on in peace and safety.

Knowing their malicious designs, I set myself to work to circumvent them; and although the wily chief counted every word dictated, and as they were marked on paper, I contrived, by joining them together, and condensing the information I gave, to warn the officer of the perfidious intentions of the savages, and tell him briefly of my helpless and unhappy captivity.

The letter was carefully examined by the chief, and the number of its apparent words recounted.

At length, appearing satisfied with its contents, he had it carried to a hill in sight of the soldier's camp, and stuck on a pole.

In due time the reply arrived, and again my ingenuity was tasked to read the answer corresponding with the number of words, that would not condemn me.

The captain's real statement was, that he distrusted all among the savages, and had great reason to.

On reading Captain Fisk's words, that seemed to

crush my already awakened hopes, my emotion overcame me.

Having told the Indians that the captain doubted their friendliness, and explained the contents of the letter as I thought best, the next day I was entrusted with the task of writing again, to solemnly assure the soldiers of the faith and friendship professed.

Again I managed to communicate with them, and this time begged them to use their field-glasses, and that I would find an excuse for standing on the hills in the afternoon, that they might see for themselves that I was what I represented myself to be—a white woman held in bondage.

The opportunity I desired was gained, and to my great delight, I had a chance of standing so as to be seen by the men of the soldier's camp.

I had given my own name in every communication. As soon as the soldiers saw that it truly was a woman of their own race, and that I was in the power of their enemies, the excitement of their feelings became so great that they desired immediately to rush to my rescue.

A gentleman belonging to the train generously offered eight hundred dollars for my ransom, which was all the money he had, and the noble, manly feeling displayed in my behalf did honor to those who felt it. There was not a man in the train who was not willing to sacrifice all he had for my rescue.

Captain Fisk restrained all hasty demonstrations,

and even went so far as to say that the first man who moved in the direction of the Indian camp should be shot immediately, his experience enabling him to know that a move of that kind would result fatally to them and to the captive.

The Indians found a box of crackers saturated with water, and, eating of them, sickened and died.

I afterward learned that some persons with the train who had suffered the loss of dear relatives and friends in the massacre of Minnesota, and who had lost their all, had poisoned the crackers with strychnine, and left them on one of their camping-grounds without the captain's knowledge.

The Indians told me afterward that more had died from eating bad bread than from bullets during the whole summer campaign.

Captain Fisk deserves great credit for his daring and courage, with his meager supply of men, against so large an army of red men.

After assurance of my presence among them, Captain Fisk proceeded to treat quietly with the savages on the subject of a ransom, offering to deliver in their village three wagon loads of stores as a price for their prisoner.

To this the deceitful creatures pretended readily to agree, and the tortured captive, understanding their tongue, heard them making fun of the credulity of white soldiers who believed their promises.

I had the use of a field-glass from the Indians, and with it I saw my white friends, which almost made me wild with excited hope.

Knowing what the Indians had planned, and dreading lest the messengers should be killed, as I knew they would be if they came to the village, I wrote to Captain Fisk of the futility of ransoming me in that way, and warned him of the treachery intended against his messengers. *

No tongue can tell or pen describe those terrible days, when, seemingly lost to hope and surrounded by drunken Indians, my life was in constant danger.

Nights of horrible revelry passed, when, forlorn and despairing, I lay listening, only half consciously, to the savage mirth and wild exultation.

To no overtures would the Indians listen, declaring I could not be purchased at any price—they were determined not to part with me. Captain Fisk and his companions were sadly disappointed in not obtaining my release, and, after a hopeless attempt, he made known the fact of my being a prisoner, spreading the news far and wide.

His expeditions across the plains had always been successful, and the Indians, knowing him to be very

* The original letters written by me to Captain Fisk are now on file in the War Department at Washington. Officially certified extracts from the correspondence are published elsewhere in this work.

brave, gave him the name of the "Great Chief, who knows no fear," and he richly deserves the appellation, for the expeditions were attended with great danger. The reports of his various expeditions have been published by Government, and are very interesting, giving a description of the country.

In September the rains were very frequent, sometimes continuing for days.

This may not seem serious to those who have always been accustomed to a dwelling and a good bed, but to me, who had no shelter and whose shrinking form was exposed to the pitiless storm, and nought but the cold ground to lie upon, bringing the pains and distress of rheumatism, it was a calamity hard to bear, and I often prayed fervently to God to give me sweet release in a flight to the land where there are no storms.

Soon the winter would be upon us, and the cold, and sleet, and stormy weather would be more difficult to bear. Would I be so fortunate, would Heaven be so gracious as to place me in circumstances where the wintry winds could not chill or make me suffer! My heart seemed faint at the thought of what was before me, for hope was lessening as winter approached!

CHAPTER XVI.

SCENES ON CANNON BALL PRAIRIE—REFLECTIONS.

WELL do I remember my thoughts and feelings when first I beheld the mighty and beautiful prairie of Cannon Ball River. With what singular emotions I beheld it for the first time! I could compare it to nothing but a vast sea, changed suddenly to earth, with all its heaving, rolling billows; thousands of acres lay spread before me like a mighty ocean, bounded by nothing but the deep blue sky. What a magnificent sight—a sight that made my soul expand with lofty thought and its frail tenement sink into utter nothingness before it! Well do I remember my sad thoughts and the turning of my mind upon the past, as I stood alone upon a slight rise of ground, and overlooked miles upon miles of the most lovely, the most sublime scene I had ever beheld. Wave upon wave of land stretched away on every hand, covered with beautiful green grass and the blooming wild flowers of the prairie. Occasionally I caught glimpses of wild animals, while flocks of birds of various kinds and beautiful plumage skimming over the surface here and there, alighting or darting upward from the earth, added life and beauty and variety to this most enchanting scene.

It had been a beautiful day, and the sun was now just burying himself in the far-off ocean of blue, and his golden rays were streaming along the surface of the waving grass and tinging it with a delightful hue. Occasionally some elevated point caught and reflected back his rays to the one I was standing upon, and it would catch, for a moment, his fading rays, and glow like a ball of golden fire. Slowly he took his diurnal farewell, as if loth to quit a scene so lovely, and at last hid himself from my view beyond the western horizon.

I stood and marked every change with that poetical feeling of pleasant sadness which a beautiful sunset rarely fails to awaken in the breast of the lover of nature. I noted every change that was going on, and yet my thoughts were far, far away. I thought of the hundreds of miles that separated me from the friends that I loved. I was recalling the delight with which I had, when a little girl, viewed the farewell scenes of day from so many romantic hills, and lakes, and rivers, rich meadows, mountain gorge and precipice, and the quiet hamlets of my dear native land so far away. I fancied I could see my mother move to the door, with a slow step and heavy heart, and gaze, with yearning affection, toward the broad, the mighty West, and sigh, wondering what had become of her lost child.

I thought, and grew more sad as I thought, until tears filled my eyes.

Mother! what a world of affection is comprised in that single word; how little do we in the giddy round of youthful pleasure and folly heed her wise counsels; how lightly do we look upon that zealous care with which she guides our otherwise erring feet, and watches with feelings which none but a mother can know the gradual expansion of our youth to the riper years of discretion. We may not think of it then, but it will be recalled to our minds in after years, when the gloomy grave, or a fearful living separation, has placed her far beyond our reach, and her sweet voice of sympathy and consolation for the various ills attendant upon us sounds in our ears no more. How deeply then we regret a thousand deeds that we have done contrary to her gentle admonitions! How we sigh for those days once more, that we may retrieve what we have done amiss and make her kind heart glad with happiness! Alas! once gone, they can never be recalled, and we grow mournfully sad with the bitter reflection.

"O, my mother!" I cried aloud, "my dearly beloved mother! Would I ever behold her again? should I ever return to my native land? Would I find her among the living? If not, if not, heavens! what a sad, what a painful thought!" and instantly I found my eyes swimming in tears and my frame trembling with nervous agitation. But I would hope for the best. Gradually I became calm; then I thought of my husband, and what might be his fate. It was sad at best, I well knew. And lastly, though I tried to avoid it, I thought of Mary; sweet, lost, but dearly beloved Mary; I could see her gentle features; I could hear her plaintive voice, soft and silvery as running waters, and sighed a long, deep sigh as I thought of her murdered. Could I never behold her again? No; she was dead, perished by the cruel, relentless savage. Silence brooded over the world; not a sound broke the solemn repose of nature; the summer breeze had rocked itself to rest in the willow boughs, and the broad-faced, familiar moon seemed alive and toiling as it climbed slowly up a cloudless sky, passing starry sentinels, whose nightly challenge was lost in vast vortices of blue as they paced their ceaseless round in the mighty camp of constellations. With my eyes fixed upon my gloomy surroundings of tyranny, occasionally a slip of moonshine silvered the ground. I watched and reflected. Oh, hallowed days of my blessed girlhood! They rise before me now like holy burning stars breaking out in a stormy, howling night, making the blackness blacker still. The short, happy springtime of life, so full of noble aspirations, and glowing hopes of my husband's philanthropic schemes of charitable projects in the future.

We had planned so much for the years to come, when, prosperous and happy, we should be able to distribute some happiness among those whose fate might be mingled with ours, and in the pursuit of our daily avocations we would find joy and peace. But, alas! for human hopes and expectations!

It is thus with our life. We silently glide along, little dreaming of the waves which will so soon sweep over us, dashing us against the rocks, or stranding us forever. We do not dream that we shall ever wreck, until the greater wave comes over us, and we bend beneath its power.

If some mighty hand could unroll the future to our gaze, or set aside the veil which enshrouds it, what pictures would be presented to our trembling hearts? No; let it be as the All-wise hath ordained—a closed-up tomb, only revealed as the events occur, for could we bear them with the fortitude we should if they were known beforehand? Shrinking from it, we would say, " Let the cup pass from me."

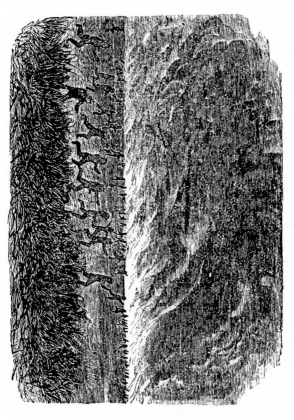

PRAIRIE ON FIRE.

Mode of Indian Burial.

CHAPTER XVII.

A PRAIRIE ON FIRE—SCENES OF TERROR.

In October, we were overtaken by a prairie fire. At this season of the year the plants and grass, parched by a hot sun, are ready to blaze in a moment if ignited by the least spark, which is often borne on the wind from some of the many camp fires.

With frightful rapidity we saw it extend in all directions, but we were allowed time to escape.

The Indians ran like wild animals from the flames, uttering yells like demons; and great walls of fire from the right hand and from the left advanced toward us, hissing, crackling, and threatening to unite and swallow us up in their raging fury.

We were amid calcined trees, which fell with a thundering crash, blinding us with clouds of smoke, and were burned by the showers of sparks, which poured upon us from all directions.

The conflagration assumed formidable proportions; the forest shrunk up in the terrible grasp of the flames, and the prairie presented one sheet of fire, in the midst of which the wild animals, driven from their dens and hiding-places by this unexpected catastrophy, ran about mad with terror.

The sky gleamed with blood-red reflection, and the impetuous wind swept both flames and smoke before it.

The Indians were terrified in the extreme on seeing around them the mountain heights lighted up like beacons, to show the entire destruction. The earth became hot, while immense troops of buffalo made the ground tremble with their furious tread, and their bellowings of despair would fill with terror the hearts of the bravest men.

Every one was frightened, running about the camp as if struck by insanity.

The fire continued to advance majestically, as it were, swallowing up every thing in its way, preceded by countless animals of various kinds, that bounded along with howls of fear, pursued by the scourge, which threatened to overtake them at every step.

A thick smoke, laden with sparks, was already passing over the camp. Ten minutes more, and all would be over with us, I thought, when I saw the squaws pressing the children to their bosoms.

The Indians had been deprived of all self-possession by the presence of our imminent peril—the flames forming an immense circle, of which our camp had become the center.

But, fortunately, the strong breeze which, up to that

moment, had lent wings to the conflagration, suddenly subsided, and there was not a breath of air stirring.

The progress of the fire slackened. Providence seemed to grant us time.

The camp presented a strange aspect. On bended knee, and with clasped hands, I prayed fervently. The fire continued to approach, with its vanguard of wild beasts.

The Indians, old and young, male and female, began to pull up the grass by the roots all about the camp, then lassoed the horses and hobbled them in the center, and, in a few moments, a large space was cleared, where the herbs and grass had been pulled up with the feverish rapidity which all display in the fear of death.

Some of the Indians went to the extremity of the space, where the grass had been pulled up, and formed a pile of grass and plants with their feet; then, with their flint, set fire to the mass, and thus caused "fire to fight fire," as they called it. This was done in different directions. A curtain of flames rose rapidly around us, and for some time the camp was almost concealed beneath a vault of fire.

It was a moment of intense and awful anxiety. By degrees the flames became less fierce, the air purer; the smoke dispersed, the roaring diminished, and, at length, we were able to recognize each other in this horrible chaos.

A sigh of relief burst from every heart. Our camp was saved! After the first moments of joy were over, the camp was put in order, and all felt the necessity of repose, after the terrible anxieties of the preceding hours; and also to give the ground time enough to cool, so that it might be traveled over by people and horses.

The next day we prepared for departure. Tents were folded, and packages were placed upon the ponies, and our caravan was soon pursuing its journey, under the direction of the chief, who rode in advance of our band.

The appearance of the prairie was much changed since the previous evening. In many places the black and burnt earth was a heap of smoking ashes; scarred and charred trees, still standing, displayed their saddening skeletons. The fire still roared at a distance, and the horizon was still obscured by smoke.

The horses advanced with caution over the uneven ground, constantly stumbling over the bones of animals that had fallen victims to the embrace of the flames.

The course we took in traveling wound along a narrow ravine, the dried bed of some torrent, deeply inclosed between two hills. The ground trodden by the horses was composed of round pebbles, which slipped from under their feet, augmenting the difficulty of the march, which was rendered still more toilsome to me by the rays of the sun falling directly upon my uncovered head and face.

The day passed away thus, and, aside from the fatigue which oppressed me, the day's journey was unbroken by any incident.

At evening, we again camped in a plain, absolutely bare; but in the distance we could see an appearance of verdure, affording great consolation, for we were about to enter a spot spared by the conflagration.

At sunrise, next morning, we were on the march toward this oasis in the desert.

CHAPTER XVIII.

MY last days with the Ogalalla Sioux Indians were destined to be marked by a terrible remembrance.

On the first of October, while the savages lingered in camp about the banks of the Yellowstone River, apparently fearing, yet almost inviting attack by their near vicinity to the soldiers, a large Mackinaw, or flat-boat, was seen coming down the river.

From their hiding-places in the rocks and bushes, they watched its progress with the stealthy ferocity of the tiger waiting for his prey.

At sundown the unsuspecting travelers pushed their boat toward the shore, and landed for the purpose of making a fire and camping for the night.

The party consisted of about twenty persons, men, women, and children. Suspecting no danger, they left their arms in the boat.

With a simultaneous yell, the savages dashed down

upon them, dealing death and destruction in rapid strokes.

The defenseless emigrants made an attempt to rush to the boat for arms, but were cut off, and their bleeding bodies dashed into the river as fast as they were slain. Then followed the torture of the women and children.

Horrible thought! from which all will turn with sickened soul, and shuddering, cry to Heaven, "How long, O Lord! how long shall such inhuman attrocities go unpunished?"

Not a soul was left alive when that black day's work was done; and the unconscious river bore away a warm tide of human blood, and sinking human forms.

When the warriors returned to camp, they brought their frightful trophies of blood-stained clothes and ghastly scalps.

My heart-sick eyes beheld the dreadful fruits of carnage; and, among the rest, I saw a woman's scalp, with heavy chestnut hair, a golden brown, and four feet in length, which had been secured for its beauty. The tempting treasure lost the poor girl her life, which might have been spared; but her glorious locks were needed to hang on the chief's belt.

Nearly all the flat-boats that passed down the Yellowstone River to the Missiouri, from the mining regions, during that season, were attacked, and in some instances one or more of the occupants killed. The approach of this boat was known, and the Indians had ample time to plan their attack so that not a soul should escape.

That night the whole camp of braves assembled to celebrate the fearful scalp dance; and from the door of my tent I witnessed the savage spectacle, for I was ill, and, to my great relief, was not forced to join in the horrid ceremony.

A number of squaws occupied the center of the ring they formed, and the pitiless wretches held up the fresh scalps that day reaped in the harvest of death.

Around them circled the frantic braves, flourishing torches, and brandishing weapons, with the most ferocious barks and yells, and wild distortions of countenance.

Some uttered boasts of bravery and prowess, and others lost their own identity in mocking their dying victims in their agony.

Leaping first on one foot, then on the other, accompanying every movement with wild whoops of excitement, they presented a scene never to be forgotten.

The young brave who bore the beautiful locks as his trophy, did not join in the dance. He sat alone, looking sad.

I approached and questioned him, and he replied that he regretted his dead victim. He brought a blood-stained dress from his lodge, and told me it was

worn by the girl with the lovely hair, whose eyes
haunted him and made him sorry.

After being cognizant of this frightful massacre, I
shrank more than ever from my savage companions,
and pursued my tasks in hopeless despondence of ever
being rescued or restored to civilized life.

One day I was astonished to notice a strange Indian,
whom I had never seen before, making signs to me of
a mysterious nature.

He indicated by signs that he wanted me to run
away with him to the white people. I had become so
suspicious, from having been deceived so many times,
that I turned from him and entered the chief's tent,
where, despite his cruelty and harshness to me, I felt
comparatively safe.

I afterward saw this Indian, or rather white man,
or half-breed, as I believe him to have been, though
he could not, or would not speak a word of English.
His long hair hung loosely about his shoulders, and
was of a dark brown color. He had in no respect the
appearance of an Indian, but rather that of a wild,
reckless frontier desperado. I had never seen him before, though he seemed well known in the camp.

One thing that perhaps made me more suspicious
and afraid to trust any one, was a knowledge of the
fact that many of the Indians who had lost relatives in
the recent battles with General Sully, were thirsting
for my blood, and would have been glad to decoy me

far enough away to wreak their vengeance, and be safe from the fury of the old chief, my task-master.

This stranger came one day into a tent where I was, and showed me a small pocket bible that had belonged to my husband, and was presented to him by his now sainted mother many years before. His object was to assure me that I might trust him; but such an instinctive horror of the man had taken possession of me that I refused to believe him; and at last he became enraged and threatened to kill me if I would not go with him.

I plead with him to give me the bible, but he refused. How dear it would have been to me from association, and what strength and comfort I would have received from its precious promises, shut out, as I was, from my world and all religious privileges and surrounded by heathen savages.

Soon after the foregoing incident, the old chief and his three sisters went away on a journey, and I was sent to live with some of his relatives, accompanied by my little companion, Yellow Bird. We traveled all day to reach our destination, a small Indian village. The family I was to live with until the return of the chief and his sisters, consisted of a very old Indian and his squaw, and a young girl.

I had a dread of going among strangers, but was thankful for the kindness with which I was received by this old couple. I was very tired, and so sad and depressed, that I cared not to ask for any thing, but the old squaw, seeming to understand my feelings, considerately placed before me meat and water, and kindly ministered to my wants in every way their means would allow.

I was with this family nearly three weeks, and was treated with almost affectionate kindness, not only by them, but by every member of the little community. The children would come to see me, and manifest in various ways their interest in me. They would say, " Wasechawea (white woman) looks sad; I want to shake hands with her."

I soon began to adapt myself to my new surroundings, and became more happy and contented than I had ever yet been since my captivity began. My time was occupied in assisting the motherly old squaw in her sewing and other domestic work.

There was but once a cloud come between us. The old chief had given orders that I was not to be permitted to go out among the other villagers alone, orders of which I knew nothing. Feeling a new sense of freedom, I had sometimes gone out, and on one occasion, having been invited into different tipis by the squaws, staid so long that the old Indian sent for me, and seemed angry when I returned. He said it was good for me to stay in his tent, but bad to go out among the others. I pacified him at last by saying I knew his home was pleasant, and I was happy there, and that I did not know it was bad to go among the other tents.

The old chief returned, finally, and my brief season of enjoyment ended. He seemed to delight in torturing me, often pinching my arms until they were black and blue. Regarding me as the cause of his wounded arm, he was determined that I should suffer with him.

While in this village "Man-Afraid-of-His-Horses" arrived, and I was made aware of his high standing as a chief and warrior by the feasting and dancing which followed. He was splendidly mounted and equipped, as also was another Indian who accompanied him.

I have since learned from my husband that the treacherous chief made such statements of his influence with the hostile Indians as to induce him to purchase for them both an expensive outfit, in the hope of my release. I saw and conversed with him several times, and though he told me that he was from the Platte, he said nothing of the real errand on which he was sent, but returned to the fort and reported to Mr. Kelly that the band had moved and I could not be found.

Captain Fisk had made known to General Sully the fact of my being among the Indians, and the efforts he had made for my release; and when the Blackfeet presented themselves before the General, asking for peace, and avowing their weariness of hostility, anxious to purchase arms, amunition, and necessaries for the approaching winter, he replied:

"I want no peace with you. You hold in captivity a white woman; deliver her up to us, and we will believe in your professions. But unless you do, we will raise an army of soldiers as numerous as the trees on the Missouri River and exterminate the Indians."

The Blackfeet assured General Sully that they held no white woman in their possession, but that I was among the Ogalallas.

"As you are friendly with them," said the General, "go to them and secure her, and we will then reward you for so doing."

The Blackfeet warriors appeared openly in the village a few days afterward, and declared their intentions, stating in council the determination of General Sully.

The Ogalallas were not afraid, they said, and refused to let me go. They held solemn council for two days, and at last resolved that the Blackfeet should take me as a ruse, to enable them to enter the fort, and a wholesale slaughter should exterminate the soldiers.

While thus deliberating as to what they thought best—part of them willing, the other half refusing to let me go—Hunkiapa, a warrior, came into the lodge, and ordered me out, immediately following me.

He then led me into a lodge where there were fifty warriors, painted and armed—their bows strung and their quivers full of arrows.

From thence, the whole party, including three
squaws, who, noting my extreme fear, accompanied me,
started toward a creek, where there were five horses
and warriors to attend us to the Blackfeet village.

Placing me on a horse, we were rapidly pursuing
our way, when a party of the Ogalallas, who were unwilling, came up with us, to reclaim me.

Here they parleyed for a time, and, finally, after a
solemn promise on the part of my new captors that I
should be returned safely, and that I should be cared
for and kindly treated, we were allowed to proceed.

In their parleying, one of the warriors ordered me
to alight from the horse, pointing a pistol to my
breast.   Many of them clamored for my life, but,
finally, they settled the matter, and permitted us to
proceed on our journey.

After so many escapes from death, this last seemed
miraculous; but God willed it otherwise, and to him I
owe my grateful homage.

It was a bitter trial for me to be obliged to go with
this new and stranger tribe.   I was unwilling to exchange my life for an unknown one, and especially as
my companionship with the sisters of the chief had
been such as to protect me from injury or insult.   A
sort of security and safety was felt in the lodge of the
chief, which now the fear of my new position made
me appreciate still more.

Savages they were, and I had longed to be free

from them; but now I parted with them with regret and misgiving.

Though my new masters, for such I considered them, held out promise of liberty and restoration to my friends, knowing the treacherous nature of the Indians, I doubted them.   True, the Ogalallas had treated me at times with great harshness and cruelty, yet I had never suffered from any of them the slightest personal or unchaste insult.   Let me bear testimony to this redeeming feature in their treatment of me.

At the time of my capture I became the exclusive property of Ottawa, the head chief, a man over seventy-five years of age, and partially blind, yet whose power over the band was absolute.   Receiving a severe wound in a melee I have already given an account of, I was compelled to become his nurse or medicine woman; and my services as such were so appreciated, that harsh and cruel as he might be, it was dangerous for others to offer me insult or injury; and to this fact, doubtless, I owe my escape from a fate worse than death.

The Blackfeet are a band of the Sioux nation; consequently, are allies in battle.   The chief dared not refuse on this account; besides, he was an invalid, and wounded badly.

The Blackfeet left three of their best horses as a guarantee for my safe return.

The chief of the Ogalallas had expressed the desire

that, if the Great Spirit should summon him away, that I might be killed, in order to become his attendant to the spirit land.

It was now the commencement of November, and their way seemed to lead to the snowy regions, where the cold might prove unendurable.

When I heard the pledge given by the Blackfeet, my fears abated; hope sprang buoyant at the thought of again being within the reach of my own people, and I felt confident that, once in the fort, I could frustrate their plans by warning the officers of their intentions.

I knew what the courage and discipline of fort soldiers could accomplish, and so hoped, not only to thwart the savage treachery, but punish the instigators.

CHAPTER XIX.

INDIAN CUSTOMS.

DURING my forced sojourn with the Ogalallas, I had abundant opportunity to observe the manners and customs peculiar to a race of people living so near, and yet of whom so little is known by the general reader. A chapter devoted to this subject will doubtless interest all who read this narrative.

Nothing can be more simple in its arrangement than an Indian camp when journeying, and especially when on the war path. The camping ground, when practicable, is near a stream of water, and adjacent to timber. After reaching the spot selected, the ponies are unloaded by the squaws, and turned loose to graze. The tents, or " tipis," are put up, and wood and water brought for cooking purposes. All drudgery of this kind is performed by the squaws, an Indian brave scorning as degrading all kinds of labor not incident to the chase or the war path.

An Indian tipi is composed of several dressed skins, usually of the buffalo, sewed together and stretched over a number of poles, the larger ones containing as many as twenty of these poles, which are fifteen to twenty feet long. They are of yellow pine, stripped of bark, and are used as "travois" in traveling. Three poles are tied together near the top or small ends, and raised to an upright position, the bottoms being spread out as far as the fastening at the top will permit. Other poles are laid into the crotch thus formed at the top, and spread out in a circular line with the three first put up. This comprises the frame work, and when in the position described is ready to receive the covering, which is raised to the top by means of a rawhide rope, when, a squaw seizing each lower corner, it is rapidly brought around, and the edges fastened together with wooden pins, a squaw getting down on all fours, forming a perch upon which the tallest squaw of the family mounts and inserts the pins as high as she can reach. A square opening in the tent serves for a door, and is entered in a stooping posture. A piece of hide hangs loosely over this opening, and is kept in position by a heavy piece of wood fastened at the bottom.

When in position, the Indian tipi is of the same shape as the Sibley tent. In the middle is built a fire, where all the cooking is done, a hole at the top affording egress for the smoke. The preparation for a meal is a very simple affair. Meat was almost their only article of diet, and was generally roasted, or rather warmed through over the fire, though sometimes it was partially boiled, and always eaten without salt or bread. They have no set time for eating; will fast all of one day, and perhaps eat a dozen times the next.

The outer edge of the tent contains the beds of the family, which are composed of buffalo robes and blankets. These are snugly rolled up during the day, and do service as seats.

If there is reason to suppose an enemy near, no fire is allowed in the camp; and in that case each one satisfies appetite as best he or she can, but generally with "pa-pa," or dried buffalo meat.

An Indian camp at close of day presents a most animated picture. The squaws passing to and fro, loaded with wood and water, or meat, or guiding the sledges drawn by dogs, carrying their all; dusky warriors squatted on the ground, in groups, around fires built in the open air, smoking their pipes, or repairing weapons, and recounting their exploits; half naked and naked children capering about in childish glee, furnish a picture of the nomadic life of these Indians of strange interest. Not more than ten minutes are required to set up an Indian village.

When it becomes necessary to move a village, which fact is never known to the people, a crier goes through the camp, shouting, "Egalakapo! Egalakapo!" when all the squaws drop whatever work they may be engaged in, and in an instant are busy as bees, taking down tipis, bringing in the ponies and dogs, and loading them; and in less than fifteen minutes the cavalcade is on the march.

The squaws accompany the men when they go to hunt buffalo, and as fast as the animals are killed, they strip off their hides, and then cut off the meat in strips about three feet long, three to four inches wide, and two inches thick; and such is their skill that the bones will be left intact and as free from meat as though they had been boiled. The meat is then taken to camp and hung up to dry. It is most filthy, being covered with grass and the excrement of the buffalo.

The medicine men treat all diseases nearly alike. The principal efforts are directed to expelling the spirit, whatever it may be, which it is expected the medicine man will soon discover, and having informed the friends what it is, he usually requires them to be in readiness to shoot it, as soon as he shall succeed in expelling it.

Incantations and ceremonies are used, intended to secure the aid of the spirit, or spirits, the Indian worships. When he thinks he has succeeded, the medicine man gives the command, and from two to six or more guns are fired at the door of the tent to destroy the spirit as it passes out.

Many of these medicine men depend wholly on conjuring, sitting by the bedside of the patient, making gestures and frightful noises, shaking rattles, and endeavoring, by all means in their power, to frighten the evil spirit. They use fumigation, and are very fond of aromatic substances, using and burning cedar and many different plants to cleanse the tent in which the sick person lies.

The native plants, roots, herbs, and so forth, are used freely, and are efficacious.

They are very careful to conceal from each other, except a few initiated, as well as from white men, a knowledge of the plants used as medicine, probably believing that their efficacy, in some measure, depends on this concealment.

There is a tall, branching plant, growing abundantly in the open woods and prairies near the Missouri River, which is used chiefly by the Indians as a purgative, and is *euphorbia corrallata*, well known to the botanist.

Medicines are generally kept in bags made of the skin of some animal.

All the drinks which are given the sick to quench thirst are astringent, sometimes bitter and sometimes slightly mucilaginous.

The most common is called red-root (*ceanothus canadensis*), a plant abounding in the western prairies, although they seem to have more faith in some ceremony.

A dance peculiar to the tribe where I was, called the pipe dance, is worth mentioning, and is called by the Indians a good medicine. A small fire is kindled in the village, and around this the dancers, which usually consist of young men, collect, each one seated upon a robe.

The presiding genius is a chief, or a medicine man, who seats himself by a fire, with a long pipe which he prepares for smoking. Offering it first to the Great Spirit, he then extends it toward the north, south, east, and west, muttering unintelligibly. Meanwhile an equally august personage beats a drum, singing and leaping and smoking. The master of ceremonies sits calmly looking on, puffing away with all the vigor imaginable.

The dance closes with piercing yells, and barking like frightened dogs, and it lasts an hour or more.

When the mother gives birth to her child, it is not uncommon for no other person to be present. She then lives in a hut or lodge by herself until the child is twenty-five or thirty days old, when she takes it to its father, who then sees his child for the first time.

Females, after parturition, and also in other conditions, bathe themselves—swim, as they express it—in the nearest river or lake.

This is, no doubt, a most efficacious means of imparting strength and vigor to the constitution, and it is certain that Indian females are less subject to what are termed female complaints than white women.

It is an uncommon occurrence that an Indian woman loses her life in parturition.

When the child is old enough to run alone, it is relieved of its swathings, and if the weather is not too cold, it is sent off without a particle of clothing to protect it or impede the action of its limbs, and in this manner it is allowed to remain until it is several years old, when it receives a limited wardrobe.

Despite the rugged and exposed life they lead, there are comparatively few cripples and deformed persons among them. It is said that deformed infants are regarded as unprofitable and a curse from the Great Spirit, and disposed of by death soon after birth. Sometimes, at the death of a mother, the infant is also interred. An incident of this kind was related to me. A whole family had been carried off by small-pox except an infant. Those who were not sick had as much to do as they could conveniently attend to, consequently there was no one willing to take charge of the little orphan. It was placed in the arms of its dead mother, enveloped in blankets and a buffalo-robe, and laid upon a scaffold in their burying-place. Its cries were heard for some time, but at last they grew fainter, and finally were hushed altogether in the cold embrace of death, with the moaning wind sounding its requiem, and the wolves howling in the surrounding gloom, a fitting dirge for so sad a fate.

The Indians believe that God, or the Great Spirit, created the universe and all things just as they exist.

They believe the sun to be a large body of heat, and that it revolves around the earth. Some believe it is a ball of fire. They do not comprehend the revolution of the earth around the sun. They suppose the sun literally rises and sets, and that our present theory is an invention of the white man, and that he is not sincere when he says the earth moves around the sun.

They say that paradise, or the happy hunting-grounds, is above, but where, they have no definite idea, though all think the future a happier state. They regard skill in hunting or success in war as the passport to eternal happiness and plenty, where there is no cold or wet season. Still they all acknowledge it is the gift of the " Wa-hon Tonka," the Great Spirit.

The manner of disposing of their dead is one of the peculiar customs of the Indians of the plains which impresses the beholder for the first time most forcibly. Four forked posts are set up, and on them a platform is laid, high enough to be out of reach of wolves or other carniverous animals, and on this the body is placed, wrapped in buffalo-robes or blankets, and sometimes both, according to the circumstances of the deceased, and these are wound securely with a strip of buffalo hide. If in the vicinity of timber, the body is placed on a platform, securely fixed in the crotch of a high tree. The wrappings of buffalo-robe or blankets protect the body from ravenous birds that hover around, attracted by the scent of an anticipated feast.

All that pertained to the dead while living, in the way of furs, blankets, weapons, cooking utensils, etc., are also deposited with the body. In some instances, the horse belonging to the deceased is shot. They believe that the spirit wanders off to distant hunting-grounds, and as it may have to pass over a country where there is no game, a quantity of dried buffalo meat is usually left with the body for its subsistence. While on a journey, these burial places are held sacred as those of a Christian nation, and when a tribe is passing such localities they will make a detour rather than go the more direct road by the resting-place of their dead, while the relatives leave the trail and go alone to the spot, and there renew and repeat their mourning as on the occasion of his death.   They also leave presents for the dead of such little trinkets as he most prized before he departed to his new hunting-grounds.

The boys are early taught the arts of war.   A bow and arrows are among the first presents that an Indian youth receives from his parents, and he is soon instructed in their use.   Indeed, the skill of a hunter seems to be a natural endowment, and, although some are more accurate and active than others, they all shoot with wonderful precision and surprising aptitude, seeming to inherit a passionate love for the sports of the chase.

The Indian boy receives no name until some distinguishing trait of character or feat suggests one, and changes it from time to time as more fitting ones are suggested.   Some of their names are very odd, and some quite vulgar.

The wife is sometimes wooed and won, as if there

was something of seatiment in the Indian character, but oftener purchased without the wooing. When the desired object is particularly attractive, and of a good family, the courting and purchasing both may be required. When a young brave goes courting, he decorates himself out in his best attire, instinctively divining that appearances weigh much in the eyes of a forest belle, or dusky maiden, who receives him bashfully, for a certain kind of modesty is inherent in Indian girls, which is rather incongruous when considered in connection with their peculiar mode of life. Discretion and propriety are carefully observed, and the lovers sit side by side in silence, he occasionally producing presents for her acceptance. These express a variety of sentiment, and refer to distinct and separate things; some signifying love; some, strength; some, bravery; others allude to the life of servitude she is expected to live if she becomes his wife. If they are accepted graciously, and the maiden remains seated, it is considered equivalent to an assurance of love on her part, and is acted upon accordingly. Although no woman's life is made less slavish by the marriage connection, and no one is treated with respect, it is scarcely known in Indian life that a girl has remained unmarried even to middle age.

When a chief desires to multiply the number of his wives, he often marries several sisters, if they can be had, not because of any particular fancy he may have for any but the one who first captivated him, but because he thinks it more likely to have harmony in the household when they are all of one family. Not even squaws can live happily together, when each may have a part interest in the same man as their husband jointly. Polygamy is inconsistent with the female character, whether in barbarism or civilization.

As many skins as they can transport on their ponies, of the game killed while on their hunts, are dressed by the squaws, and then taken to some trading post, military station, or agency, and bartered off for such articles as are most desired by them, such as beads, paints, etc., and powder, lead, and caps. They are willing to allow much more proportionately for ammunition than any other articles. They are most outrageously swindled by the traders whom our Government licenses to trade with them. A buffalo-robe which the trader sells for from ten to fifteen dollars, is bought from the Indians for a pint cup of sugar and a small handful of bullets, while furs of all kinds are exchanged for paints and trinkets at equally disproportionate rates. The Indians know they are cheated whenever they barter with the white traders, but they have no remedy, as there is no competition, and hence much of their disaffection.

Buffalo-robes, bearskins, and deer, and antelope skins are brought in in great numbers; they shoot and trap the beaver and otter expressly for their furs.

The Indians are almost universally fond of whisky,

and have a strong propensity for gambling. They will risk at cards almost every thing they own, and if unsuccessful appear quite resigned to their loss, resting in the gambler's hope of "better luck next time."

The squaws play a game with small bones of oblong shape, which seems to have a great fascination for them, as I have known them to spend whole days and nights at it, and in many instances gambling away every thing they owned. Five of these pieces are used, each possessing a relative value in the game, designated by spots from one to five on one side, the other being blank. They are placed in a dish or small basket, which is shaken and then struck upon the ground with a jar, tossing the pieces over, and according to the number of spots up, so is the game decided, very similar, I imagine, to the white man's game of "high-die."

They have a peculiar way of defining time. When they wish to designate an hour of the day, they point to the position the sun should be in at that time. The number of days is the number of sleeps. Their next division of time is the number of moons, instead of our months; and the seasons are indicated by the state of vegetation. For instance, spring is when the grass begins to grow, and the autumn when the leaves fall from the trees, while years are indicated by the season of snows.

There is a language of signs common to all the tribes,

by which one tribe may communicate with another without being able to speak or understand its dialect. Each tribe is known by some particular sign.

The Indian is noted for his power of endurance of both fatigue and physical pain. I have thought much upon the fear manifested by these reputed brave barbarians; they seem to be borne down with the most tormenting fear for their personal safety at all times, at home or roaming for plunder, or when hunting, and yet courage is made a virtue among them, while cowardice is the unpardonable sin. When compelled to meet death, they seem to muster sullen, obstinate defiance of their doom, that makes the most of a dreaded necessity, rather than seek a preparation to meet it with submission, which they often dissemble, but never possess.

Instinct, more than reason, is the guide of the red man. He repudiates improvement, and despises manual effort. For ages has his heart been imbedded in moral pollution.

The blanket, as worn by the Indian, is an insuperable barrier to his advance in arts or agriculture. When this is forever dispensed with, then his hands will be free to grasp the mechanic's tools or guide the plow. It is both graceful and chaste in their eyes, and to adopt the white man's dress is a great obstacle, a requirement too humiliating, for they have personal as well as national pride. No hat is worn, but the head is covered with feathers aud rude ornaments. A heavy mass of wampum, often very expensive, adorns the neck. Frequently the entire rim of each ear is pierced with holes, and adorned with jewels of silver, or something resembling it.

The Indian does every thing through motives of policy. He has none of the kindlier feelings of humanity in him. He is as devoid of gratitude as he is hypocritical and treacherous. He observes a treaty, or promise, only so long as it is dangerous for him to disregard it, or for his interest, in other ways, to keep it. Cruelty is inherent in them, and is early manifested in the young, torturing birds, turtles, or any little animal that may fall into their hands. They seem to delight in it, while the pleasure of the adult in torturing his prisoners is most unquestionable. They are inveterate beggars, but never give, unless with a view to receive a more valuable present in return.

The white man, he has been taught, is his enemy, and he has become the most implacable enemy of the white man. His most fiendish murders of the innocent is his sweetest revenge for a wrong that has been done by another.

The youth are very fond of war. They have no other ambition, and pant for the glory of battle, longing for the notes of the war song, that they may rush in and win the feathers of a brave. They listen to the stories of the old men, as they recall the stirring scenes of their youth, or sing their war songs, which form only a boasting recapitulation of their daring and bravery. They yearn for the glory of war, which is the only path to distinction. Having no arts or industrial pursuits, the tribes are fast waning from war, exposure, and disease.

But few of the tribes cultivate the soil, the nature of the Indian rendering in his eyes as degrading all labor not incident to the chase or the war-path; and notwithstanding the efforts of missionaries, and the vast sums of money expended by the Government to place them on reservations and teach them the art of agriculture, the attempts to civilize the Indian in that way may be considered almost a total failure. The results bear no comparison to their cost.

Their ideas of the extent and power of the white race are very limited, and after I had learned the language sufficiently to converse with them, I frequently tried to explain to them the superior advantages of the white man's mode of living. They would ask me many questions, as to the number of the white men on this side of the big water, and how far that extended; and on being told of two big oceans, they would ask if the whites owned the big country on the other side, and if there were any Indians there. Many of my statements were received with incredulity, and I was often called a liar, especially when I told of the number and rapid increase of the white race; sometimes the older ones would get angry. The younger ones were often eager listeners, and especially in times of scarcity and hunger would they gather around me to learn about the white man, and then would I endeavor to impress them with the advantages of a fixed home and tilling the soil over their wild, roaming life.

CHAPTER XX.

AN INDIAN TRADITION—ARRIVAL AT THE BLACKFEET VILLAGE—AN OFFER TO PURCHASE ME INDIGNANTLY REJECTED—A YANKTON ATTEMPTS MY CAPTURE.

THE Blackfeet village was one hundred and fifty miles from the Ogalallas, and the way thither lay often over the tops of bare and sandy hills.

On the summits of these heights I found shells such as are picked up at the sea-side. The Indians accounted for their appearance there by saying, that once a great sea rolled over the face of the country, and only one man in a boat escaped with his family. He had sailed about in the boat until the waters retired to their place, and, living there, became the father of all the Indians.

These savages proved very kind to me. Though their nation is regarded by the whites as very vindictive and hostile, they showed me nothing but civility and respect.

On the third morning we reached a small village, where we halted. The Indians of the village were rejoiced to see me. Among them I recognized many familiar faces, and they imparted to us their mistrust and apprehension lest I had been stolen from the Ogalallas; but the Blackfeet assured them to the contrary; and, after questioning me, they became satisfied, and gave us food, promising to send warriors to our village, and giving us another horse.

The journey to the village of the Blackfeet was exceedingly wearisome—completely exhausting me by its length; and I suffered from the intense cold weather.

Approaching their village, they entered it with loud demonstrations of joy, singing and whooping after the manner of their race, with noises defying description.

I was received with great joy; and even marks of distinction were shown me. That night there was a feast, and every thing denoted a time of rejoicing.

My life was now changed—instead of waiting upon others, they waited upon me.

The day of my arrival in the Blackfeet village was a sad one, indeed, being the first anniversary of my wedding. The songs and shouts of exultation of the Indians seemed like a bitter mockery of my misery and helplessness.

I met in the village many warriors whom I had seen during the summer, and knew that they had participated in the battles with General Sully. They saw that something had made me sad and thoughtful, and asked what it was. I told them it was my birth-day.

Soon after my arrival, Egosegalonicha was sent to me, and inquired how I was treated, and particularly wished to know if they were respectful to me. She told me that she was sent to inquire for my safety and well-being, and that any remissness on the part of the Blackfeet would be visited with vengeance.

She told me that her people mourned the captive's absence, and grieved for her presence. From others I learned the same.

Next morning there was great commotion in the camp, caused by the arrival of a delegation from the Yanktons, with a handsome horse and saddle, as a present for me.

The saddle was of exquisite workmanship, embroidered with beads, and richly decorated with fringe.

The Yanktons desired to purchase me, offering five of their finest horses for me, which the Blackfeet were quite indignant at, replying, that they also had fine horses; and, deeming it an insult, returned the horse and its saddle. Fearing my disappointment, they, in council that night, decided to present me with something as worthy as the Yanktons had sent.

Accordingly, at the door of the tent next morning were four of their best animals; eight beautiful robes were brought in by the young men, and given me also.

The Yanktons were told to return to their tribe, and if such a message was again sent, the hatchet would be painted and given to them

This closed the negotiation, but not their efforts to obtain me.

The large reward which had been offered for my recovery caused the Indians much trouble, as frequently large parties from other tribes would come in, offering to purchase me from those who held me captive. Several such instances occurred while I was with the Ogalallas; nor were the Blackfeet exempt from similar annoyances.

One day, while in Tall Soldier's tipi, there was a large body of mounted warriors seen approaching the village. The women gathered around me, and told me I must stay in the tent, concealed. All was excitement, and the women seemed frightened. Soon I knew that preparations were being made for a feast on a large scale. The strange warriors came into camp and held a council, at which Tall Soldier made a speech, which, from the distance, I could not understand; they then had a feast, and departed. The Blackfeet gave me to understand that the visit of these Indians was on my account, as had been that of the Yanktons.

Soon after, I noticed that parties of warriors would leave the camp daily and return, bringing ammunition and goods of various kinds. I learned from the squaws and children that a party of traders from the Platte River had arrived in the neighborhood with four wagons, to trade with the Indians, and that they wanted to buy me, but that the Indians would not part with me. I pretended to the Indians that I did not desire to leave them, but plead that I might go with them to see the white men, which was refused, as was also a request that I might write a letter to them.

Soon after, the traders were murdered, only one man escaping, who reached Fort Laramie nearly dead from hunger and exposure, having traveled the whole distance from the Missouri River on foot.

I have since learned that the men were sent out by Mr. Beauve, a trader, near Fort Laramie, with instructions to procure my release if it required all they possessed.

Since learning these facts, I am more than ever convinced that the reluctance of the Indians to give me up grew out of their hope of capturing Fort Sully through my involuntary agency, and securing a greater booty than any ransom offered; as also of obtaining revenge for the losses inflicted upon their nation by the soldiers under General Sully.

The Blackfeet appeared in every respect superior to the tribe I had left. The chief, "Tall Soldier," displayed the manners and bearing of a natural gentleman.

They kept up an air of friendliness, and communicated frequently with the whites; but, in reality, were ready to join any hostile expedition against them, and were with the Ogalalla Sioux when our train was attacked at Box Elder.

The Blackfeet seemed to be stationary in their village, only sallying out in small parties for plunder and horses; and, during that time, keeping up a succession of entertainments at the tipi of the chief, where a constant arrival of warriors and many Indians from other tribes, who were warmly welcomed, added to the excitement of the days.

I sympathized with the poor wife of the chief, who was the only woman, beside myself, in the tent, and to whose labor all the feasts were due.

She was obliged to dress the meat, make fires, carry water, and wait upon strangers, besides setting the lodge in order.

These unceasing toils she performed alone—the commands of the chief forbidding me to aid her.

While with the Ogalallas, I had never crossed their will or offered resistance to my tasks, however heavy, having learned that obedience and cheerful industry were greatly prized; and it was, doubtless, my conciliating policy that had at last won the Indians, and made them bewail my loss so deeply.

The squaws are very rebellious, often displaying ungovernable and violent temper. They consider their life a servitude, and being beaten at times like animals, and receiving no sort of sympathy, it acts upon them accordingly.

The contrast between them and my patient submission had its effect upon the Indians, and caused them to miss me when separated from them.

During my sojourn in this village I received invitations to every feast, and to the different lodges. One day, when visiting one of these lodges, a package of letters was given me to read. They had been taken from Captain Fisk's train, and were touchingly beautiful. Some of them were the correspondence of a Mr. Nichols with a young lady, to whom he seemed tenderly attached. I was asked to read these letters and explain them to the Indians.

I was removed at different times to various lodges, as a sort of concealment, as I learned that the Yanktons had not yet given up the idea of securing me; and, one night, I awoke from my slumbers to behold an Indian bending over me, cutting through the robes which covered me, after making a great incision in the tent, whereby he entered. Fearing to move, I reached out my hand to the sqnaw who slept near me (whose name was Chahompa Sca—White Sugar), pinching her, to arouse her, which had its effect; for she immediately arose and gave the alarm, at which the Indian fled. This caused great excitement in the camp, and many threats were made against the Yanktons.

The intense cold and furious storms that followed my arrival among the Blackfeet precluded the possibility of their setting out immediately on the proposed journey to Fort Sully.

The snow-drifts had rendered the mountain passes impassable, and the chief informed me that they must wait until they were free from danger, before taking leave of the shelter and security of their protected village.

Jumping Bear Promising by the Moon, to Carry My Letter to the
White Chief at Fort Sully.

My Arrival at Fort Sully.

CHAPTER XXI.

APPEARANCE OF JUMPING BEAR — I PREVAIL ON HIM TO CARRY A
LETTER TO THE FORT—A WAR SPEECH—INTENDED TREACHERY—
RESUME OUR JOURNEY TO THE FORT—SINGULAR MEETING WITH A
WHITE MAN — "HAS RICHMOND FALLEN ? "—ARRIVAL AT THE
FORT—I AM FREE!

"JUMPING BEAR," who rescued me from the revengeful arrow of the Indian whose horse the chief
shot, one day presented himself to me, and reminded
me of my indebtedness to him in thus preserving my
life.

Trembling with fear, I listened to his avowal of
more than ordinary feeling, during which he assured
me that I had no cause to fear him—that he had
always liked the white woman, and would be more
than a friend to me.

I replied, that I did not fear him; that I felt grateful to him for his kindness and protection, but that
unless he proved his friendship for me, no persuasion
could induce me to listen.

"Will you carry a letter to my people at the fort,
delivering it into the hands of the great chief there?
They will reward you for your kindness to their sister;

they will give you many presents, and you will return rich."

"I dare not go," he replied. "Nor could I get back before the warriors came to our village."

"My people will give you a fast horse," said I, "and you may return speedily. Go now, and prove your friendship by taking the letter, and returning with your prizes."

I assured him that the letter contained nothing that would harm him or his people; that I had written of him and of his kindness, and of his good will toward them. After many and long interviews, the women of the lodge using their influence, I at last prevailed upon him to go, and invoking the bright moon as a witness to my pledge of honor and truth, he started on his journey, bearing the letter, which I believed was to seal my fate for weal or wo. In the moonlight I watched his retreating form, imploring Heaven to grant the safe delivery of the little messenger, upon which so much depended.

Daring and venturesome deed! Should he prove false to me, and allow any one outside the fort to see the letter, my doom was inevitable.

Many days of intense anxiety were passed after his departure. The squaws, fearing that I had done wrong in sending him, were continually asking questions, and it was with difficulty I could allay their

anxiety, and prevent them from disclosing the secret
to the other women.

The contents of the letter were a warning to the
"Big Chief" and the soldiers of an intended attack
on the fort and the massacre of the garrison, using me
as a ruse to enable them to get inside the fort; and
beseeching them to rescue me if possible.

The messenger reached the fort, and was received
by the officer of the day, Lieutenant Hesselberger, and
conducted to the commander of the post, Major House,
and Adjutant Pell, who had been left there to treat
with the Indians on my account.*

General Sully was absent at Washington, but every
necessary precaution was taken to secure the fort.

Jumping Bear received a suit of clothes and some
presents, and was sent back with a letter for me, which
I never received, as I never saw him again. These
facts I learned after my arrival at Fort Sully.

The night before our departure from the Blackfeet
village, en route for the fort, I was lying awake, and
heard the chief address his men seriously upon the
subject of their wrongs at the hands of the whites. I
now understood and spoke the Indian tongue readily,.

---

* A written statement from Lieutenant Hesselberger, setting
forth the fact of my writing and sending the letter of warning,
and that it undoubtedly was the means of saving the garrison at
Fort Sully from massacre, is on file in the Treasury Department
at Washington. A certified copy is published in connection with
this narrative.

and so comprehended his speech, which, as near as I can recollect, was as follows:

" Friends and sons, listen to my words. You are a great and powerful band of our people. The inferior race, who have encroached on our rights and territories, justly deserve hatred and destruction. These intruders came among us, and we took them by the hand. We believed them to be friends and true speakers; they have shown us how false and cruel they can be.

" They build forts to live in and shoot from with their big guns. Our people fall before them. Our game is chased from the hills. Our women are taken from us, or won to forsake our lodges, and wronged and deceived.

" It has only been four or five moons since they drove us to desperation, killed our brothers and burned our tipis. The Indian cries for vengeance! There is no truth nor friendship in the white man; deceit and bitterness are in his words.

" Meet them with equal cunning. Show them no mercy. They are but few, we are many. Whet your knives and string your bows; sharpen the tomahawk and load the rifle.

" Let the wretches die, who have stolen our lands, and we will be free to roam over the soil that was our fathers'. We will come home bravely from battle

Our songs shall rise among the hills, and every tipi shall be hung with the scalp-locks of our foes."

This declaration of hostilities was received with grunts of approval; and silently the war preparations went on, that I might not know the evil design hidden beneath the mask of friendship.

That night, as if in preparation for the work he had planned, the gracious chief beat his poor tired squaw unmercifully, because she murmured at her never-ending labor and heavy tasks.

His deportment to me was as courteous as though he had been educated in civilized life; indeed, had he not betrayed so much ignorance of the extent and power of the American nation, in his address to his band, I should have thought him an educated Indian, who had traveled among the whites. Yet in his brutal treatment of his squaw, his savage nature asserted itself, and reminded me that, although better served than formerly, I was still among savages.

When morning came to my sleepless night, I arose, still dreading lest some terrible intervention should come between me and the longed-for journey to the abodes of white men.

The day before leaving the Blackfeet village, I gave all my Indian trinkets to a little girl who had been my constant companion, and by her gentle and affectionate interest in the captive white woman, had created within me a feeling akin to love. She was half white, and was grand-daughter of a chief called Wichunkiapa, who also treated me with kindness.

The morning after the chief's address to his warriors, the savages were all ready for the road, and, mounting in haste, set up their farewell chant as they wound in a long column out of the village.

I have frequently been asked, since my restoration to civilization, how I dressed while with the Indians, and whether I was clothed as the squaws were. A description of my appearance as I rode out of the Indian village that morning, will satisfy curiosity on this point.

My dress consisted of a narrow white cotton gown, conposed of only two breadths, reaching below the knee, and fastened at the waist with a red scarf; moccasins, embroidered with beads and porcupine quills, covered my feet, and a robe over my shoulders completed my wardrobe.

While with the Ogalallas, I wore on my arms great brass rings that had been forced on me, some of them fitting so tight that they lacerated my arms severely, leaving scars that I shall ever retain as mementos of my experience in Indian ornamentation. I was also painted as the squaws were, but never voluntarily applied the article.

It was winter, and the ground was covered with snow, but so cold was the air that its surface bore the horses' feet on its hard, glittering breast, only breaking through occasionally in the deep gullies.

It was two hundred miles from the Blackfeet village to Fort Sully, in the middle of winter, and the weather intensely cold, from the effects of which my ill-clad body suffered severely. I was forced to walk a great part of the way, to keep from freezing. Hoping for deliverance, yet dreading lest the treacherous plans of the Indians for the capture of the fort and massacre of its garrison might prove successful, and my return to captivity inevitable, I struggled on, striving to bear with patience the mental and bodily ills from which I suffered. My great fear was that my letter had not fallen into the right hands.

On our journey we came in sight of a few lodges, and in among the timber we camped for the night. While in one of the lodges, to my surprise, a gentlemanly figure approached me, dressed in modern style. It astonished me to meet this gentlemanly-looking, well-mannered gentleman under such peculiar circumstances. He drew near and addressed me courteously.

"This is cold weather for traveling. Do you not find it so?" he inquired.

"Not when I find myself going in the right direction," I replied.

I asked him if he lived in that vicinity, supposing, of course, from the presence of a white man in our camp, that we must be near some fort, trading-post, or white settlement.

He smiled and said, "I am a dweller in the hills, and confess that civilized life has no charms for me. I find in freedom and nature all the elements requisite for happiness."

Having been separated from the knowledge and interests of national affairs just when the struggle agitating our country was at its height, I asked the question:

"Has Richmond been taken?"

"No, nor never will be," was the reply.

Further conversation on national affairs convinced me that he was a rank rebel.

We held a long conversation, on various topics. He informed me he had lived with the Indians fourteen years; was born in St. Louis, had an Indian wife, and several children, of whom he was very proud; and he seemed to be perfectly satisfied with his mode of living.

I was very cautious in my words with him, lest he might prove a traitor; but in our conversation some Indian words escaped my lips, which, being overheard, rumor construed into mischief. What I had said was carried from lodge to lodge, increasing rather than diminishing, until it returned to the lodge where I was. The Indians, losing confidence in me, sent the young men, at midnight, to the camp of the white man, to ascertain what had been said by me, and my feelings toward them.

He assured the messengers that I was perfectly friendly, had breathed nothing but kindliness for them, and was thoroughly contented; had so expressed myself, and there was no cause to imagine evil.

This man trafficked and traded with the Indians, disposing of his goods in St. Louis and in eastern cities, and was then on his way to his home, near the mouth of the Yellowstone River.

Early in the forenoon of the last day's travel, my eager and anxious eyes beheld us nearing the fort. The Indians paused and dismounted to arrange their dress and see to the condition of their arms. Their blankets and furs were adjusted; bows were strung, and the guns examined by them, carefully. They then divided into squads of fifties, several of these squads remaining in ambush among the hills, for the purpose of intercepting any who might escape the anticipated massacre at the fort; the others then rode on toward the fort, bearing me with them.

A painfully startling sight (the last I was destined to see), here met my gaze. One of the warriors, in passing, thrust out his hand to salute me. It was covered by one of my husband's gloves, and the sight of such a memento filled me with inexpressible dread as to his fate. Nothing in the least way connected with him had transpired to throw any light upon his whereabouts, or whether living or dead, since we had been so suddenly and cruelly separated. All was darkness and doubt concerning him.

Mr. Kelly had been a Union soldier, and happening to have his discharge papers with me at the time of my capture, I had been able to secrete them ever since, treasuring them merely because they had once belonged to him and contained his name.

Now, as we approached the place where his fate would be revealed to me, and, if he lived, we would meet once more, the appearance of that glove, on the savage hand, was like a touch that awakened many chords, some to thrill with hope, some to jar painfully with fear.

In appearance I had suffered from my long estrangement from home life. I had been obliged to paint daily, like the rest of my companions, and narrowly escaped tattooing, by pretending to faint away every time the implements for the marring operation were applied.

During the journey, whenever an opportunity offered, I would use a handful of snow to cleanse my cheeks from savage adornment; and now, as we drew nearer the fort, and I could see the chiefs arranging themselves for effect, my heart beat high, and anticipation became so intense as to be painful.

Eight chiefs rode in advance, one leading my horse by the bridle, and the warriors rode in the rear. The cavalcade was imposing. As we neared the fort they raised the war song, loud and wild, on the still, wintry air; and, as if in answer to its notes, the glorious flag of our country was run up, and floated bravely forth on the breeze from the tall flag-staff within the fort.

My eyes caught the glad sight, and my heart gave a wild bound of joy; something seemed to rise in my throat and choke my breathing Every thing was changed; the torture of suspense, the agony of fear, and dread of evil to come, all seemed to melt away like mist before the morning sunshine, when I beheld the precious emblem of liberty. How insignificant and contemptible in comparison were the flaunting Indian flags that had so long been displayed to me; and how my heart thrilled with a sense of safety and protection as I saw the roofs of the buildings within the fort covered by the brave men who composed that little garrison.

The precious emblem of liberty, whose beloved stripes and stars floated proudly out, seemed to beckon me to freedom and security; and as the fresh breeze stirred its folds, shining in the morning light, and caused them to wave lightly to and fro, they came like the smile of love and the voice of affection, all combined, to welcome me to home and happiness once more.

An Indian hanger-on of the fort had sauntered carelessly forward a few minutes previous, as if actuated by curiosity, but in reality to convey intelligence to his fellow-savages of the state of the fort and its defenses.

Then the gate was opened, and Major House appeared, accompanied by several officers and an interpreter, and received the chiefs who rode in advance.

Meanwhile, Captain Logan (the officer of the day), a man whose kind and sympathetic nature did honor to his years and rank, approached me. My emotions were inexpressible, now that I felt myself so nearly rescued. At last they overcame me. I had borne grief and terror and privation; but the delight of being once more among my people was so overpowering that I almost lost the power of speech, or motion, and when I faintly murmured, "Am I free, indeed free?" Captain Logan's tears answered me as well as his scarcely uttered "Yes," for he realized what freedom meant to one who had tasted the bitterness of bondage and despair.

As soon as the chiefs who accompanied me entered the gate of the fort, the commandant's voice thundered the order for them to be closed.

The Blackfeet were shut out, and I was beyond their power to recapture.

After a bondage lasting more than five months, during which I had endured every torture, I once more stood free, among people of my own race, all ready to assist me, and restore me to my husband's arms.

Three ladies, residing at the fort, received me, and cheerfully bestowed every care and attention which could add to my comfort and secure my recovery from the fatigues and distresses of my past experience.

CHAPTER XXII.

RETROSPECTION—A BORDER TRADING POST—GARRISON HOSPITALITY—
A VISIT FROM THE COMMANDANT OF FORT RICE—ARRIVAL OF
MY HUSBAND—AFFECTING SCENE.

AT first, and some time afterward, at intervals, the effects of my life among the savages preyed upon my mind so as to injure its quiet harmony. I was ill at ease among my new friends, and they told me that my eyes wore a strangely wild expression, like those of a person constantly in dread of some unknown alarm.

Once more free and safe among civilized people, I looked back on the horrible past with feelings that defy description.

The thought of leaving this mortal tenement on the desert plain for the wolves to devour, and the bones to bleach under the summer sun and winter frosts, had been painful indeed. Now, I knew that if the wearied spirit should leave its earthly home, the body would be cared for by kind Christian friends, and tenderly laid beneath the grass and flowers, and my heart rejoiced therein.

Hunger and thirst, long days of privation and

suffering, had been mine. No friendly voices cheered me on; all was silence and despair. But now the scene had changed, and the all-wise Being, who is cognizant of every thought, knew the joy and gratitude of my soul.

True, during the last few weeks of my captivity, the Indians had done all in their power for me, all their circumstances and condition would allow, and the women were very kind, but "their people were not my people," and I was detained a captive, far from home, and friends, and civilization.

With Alexander Selkirk I could say, "Better dwell in the midst of alarms, than reign in this horrible place."

Being young, and possessed of great cheerfulness and elasticity of temper, I was enabled to bear trials which seemed almost impossible for human nature to endure and live.

Soon after my arrival at the fort, Captain Pell came and invited me to go to a trader's store to obtain a dress for myself. I needed it very much, having no clothing of my own to wear.

A kind lady, Mrs. Davis, accompanied me, and the sight that presented itself to my wondering eyes will never be erased from memory.

By the door-steps, on the porches, and every-where, were groups of hungry Indians of all sizes and both sexes, claiming to be friendly.

Some of them were covered with every conceivable

kind of superficial clothing and adornment, and critically wanting in cleanliness, a peculiar trait among the Indians of the Northwest.

There was the papoose, half-breeds of any number, a few absolutely nude, others wrapped slightly in bits of calico, a piece of buckskin, or fur.

Speculators, teamsters, and interpreters, mingled with the soldiers of the garrison—squaws, with their bright, flashing shawls, or red cloth, receiving, in their looped-up blanket, the various articles of border traffic, such as sugar, rice, flour, and other things—tall warriors bending over the same counter, purchasing tobacco, brass nails, knives, and glass beads, all giving words to thought, and a stranger might well wonder which was the better prototype of tongues. The Cheyennes supplement their words with active and expressive gestures, while the Sioux amply use their tongues as well as their arms and fingers.

To all, whether half-breed, Indian, or white man, the gentlemanly trader gave kind and patient attention, while himself and clerks seemed ready and capable of talking Sioux, French, or English, just as the case came to hand.

It was on the 12th of December when I reached the fort, and like heaven the place appeared after the trials of savage life.

The officers and men were like brothers to me; and their tender sympathy united me to them in the

strongest bonds of friendship, which not even death
can sever.

A party and supper was made for my special benefit,
and on New Year's morning I was serenaded with cannon. Every attention and kindness was bestowed upon
me; and to Dr. John Ball, post surgeon, I owe a debt
of gratitude which mere words can never express. He
was my attendant physician during my sojourn at the
fort, and, as my physical system had undergone very
severe changes, I needed great care. Under his skillful treatment and patient attention I soon recovered
health and strength. I had been severely frozen on
the last days of my journey with the Indians toward
the fort.

Colonel Diamond, from Fort Rice, came to visit me
ere I left Fort Sully. He was attended by an escort
of one hundred and eighty men.

He told me of his efforts to obtain my release, and
that he, with his men, had searched the Indian village
for me, but found no warriors there, as they had
already taken me to the fort. The Indian women
had made him understand by signs that the "White
Woman" had gone with the chiefs.

He said the Indians were so enraged about giving
me up, that they killed three of his men and scalped
them, by orders from the chief, Ottawa, who was unable to do any service himself, being a cripple. He
bade them bring him the scalps of the white men.

An Indian, who killed one of the men, fell dead in his lodge the same day, which frightened his people not a little; for, in their superstition, they deemed it a visitation of the Great Spirit for a wrong done.

Colonel Diamond did not forget me, neither did he cease in his efforts in my behalf.

During all this time no tidings had been received by me of my husband. But one day, great commotion was occasioned in the fort by the announcement that the mail ambulance was on the way to the fort, and would reach it in a few moments. An instant after, a soldier approached me, saying: "Mrs. Kelly, I have news for you. Your husband is in the ambulance."

No person can have even a faint idea of the uncontrollable emotions which swept over me like an avalanche at that important and startling news. But it was not outwardly displayed. The heart-strings were stirred to their utmost depths, but gave no sound. Trembling, quivering in their strong feeling, they told not of the deep grief and joy intermingled there.

Mechanically, I moved around, awaiting the presence of the beloved, and was soon folded to his breast, where he held me with a grasp as if fearful of my being torn from him again.

Not an eye present but was suffused with tears. Soldiers and men, the ladies who had been friends to me, all mingled their tears and prayers. Language fails to describe our meeting. For seven long months we had not beheld each other, and the last time was on the terrible field of slaughter and death.

His personal appearance, oh! how changed! His face was very pale, and his brown hair was sprinkled with gray. His voice was alone unchanged. He called me by name, and it never sounded so sweet before. His very soul seemed imbued with sadness at our separation, and the terrible events which caused it.

My first question was concerning my little Mary; for her fate had been veiled in mystery. He gave me the account of her burial—a sad and heart-rending story, sufficient to chill the lightest heart—which account comprises the succeeding chapter.

CHAPTER XXIII.

SAD FATE OF LITTLE MARY.

THE reader will please go back with me to that fearful first night of my captivity, and to the moment when I put into execution the plan for dear little Mary's escape, which I prayed might result in her restoration to our friends.

It must have been something more than a vague hope of liberty to be lost or won that guided the feeble steps of the child back on the trail to a bluff overlooking the road where, weary from the fatigue and terror of a night passed alone on the prairie, she sat, anxious, but hopeful, awaiting the coming of friends.

Rescue was seemingly near, now that she had reached the great road, and she knew that there would be a passing train of emigrants ere long.

It was in this situation she was seen by some passing soldiers, holding out her little trembling hands with eager joy and hope, imploring them to save her.

It was a party of but three or four soldiers returning from Fort Laramie, where they had been to meet the paymaster. They had been pursued by Indians the day before; had also passed the scene of the destruction of our train; and believed the country swarming with Indians. Their apprehensions were, therefore, fully aroused, and, fearing the little figure upon the distant bluff might be a decoy to lead them into ambush, hesitated to approach. There was a large ravine between, and it is not strange that their imagination should people it with lurking savages. However, they were about crossing to the relief of the little girl, when a party of Indians came in sight, and they became convinced it was a decoy, and turned and fled.

They returned to Deer Creek Station, and related the circumstance. Mr. Kelly, arriving soon after, heard it, and his heart sank within him at the description of the child, for he thought he recognized in it the form of our little Mary.

He applied to the officer in command for a detail of soldiers to go with him to search for her, but all entreaty and argument were in vain.

The agony that poor child endured as the soldiers turned away, and the war-whoop of the savage rang upon her terrified soul, is known only to God. Instead of the rescue and friends which, in her trusting heart and innocent faith, she had expected to find, fierce Indians stood before her, stringing their bows to take her life, thus to win another trophy, marking the Indian murderer.

The whizzing arrows were sent into the body of the helpless child, and with the twang of the bow-strings, the delicate form of the heroic child lay stretched upon the ground, and the bright angel spirit went home to rest in the bosom of its Father.

On the morning of the 14th, two days after Mary was seen, Mr. Kelly succeeded in obtaining a squad of soldiers at the station, and went out to search for the child, and after a short march of eight miles, they discovered the mutilated remains of the murdered girl.

Mr. Kelly's grief and anguish knew no bounds.

Three arrows had pierced the body, and the tomahawk and scalping-knife had done their work. When discovered, her body lay with its little hands outstretched as if she had received, while running, the fatal arrows.

Surely He who numbers the sparrows and feeds the ravens was not unmindful of her in that awful hour, but allowed the heavenly kingdom, to which her trembling soul was about to take its flight, to sweeten, with a glimpse of its beatific glory, the bitterness of death, even as the martyr Stephen, seeing the bliss above, could not be conscious of the torture below.

Extracting the arrows from the wounds, and dividing her dress among the soldiers, then tenderly wrapping her in a winding sheet, Mr. Kelly had the sad satisfaction of smoothing the earth on the unconscious breast that had ceased to suffer, and when this duty was performed, they left the little grave all alone, far from the happy home of her childhood, and the brothers, with whom she had played in her innocent joy.

Of all strange and terrible fates, no one who had seen her gentle face in its loving sweetness, the joy and comfort of our hearts, would have predicted such a barbarous fate for her. But it was only the passage from death into life, from darkness into daylight, from doubt and fear into endless love and joy. Those little ones, whose spirits float upward from their downy pillows, amid the tears and prayers of broken-hearted friends, are blest to enter in at heaven's shining gate, which lies as near little Mary's rocky, blood-stained pillow in the desolate waste as the palace of a king, and when she had once gained the great and unspeakable bliss of heaven, it must have blotted out the remembrance of the pain that won it, and made no price too great for such delight.

> In the far-off land of Indian homes,
>   Where western winds fan " hills of black,"
> 'Mid lovely flowers, and golden scenes,
>   They laid our loved one down to rest.
>
> Where brightest birds, with silvery wings,
>   Sing their sweet songs upon her grave,
> And the moonbeam's soft and pearly beams
>   With prairie grasses o'er it wave.
>
> No simple stone e'er marks the spot
>   Where Mary sleeps in dreamless sleep,

But the moaning wind, with mournful sound,
  Doth nightly o'er it vigils keep.

The careless tread of savage feet,
  And the weary travelers, pass it by,
Nor heed they her, who came so far
  In her youth and innocence to die.

But her happy spirit soared away
  To blissful climes above;
She found sweet rest and endless joy
  In her bright home of love.

CHAPTER XXIV.

WHAT OCCURRED AT FORT LARAMIE AFTER MY CAPTURE—EFFORTS TO
RESCUE—LIEUTENANT BROWN KILLED—REWARD OFFERED—IT IS
THE MEANS OF RESTORING ANOTHER WHITE WOMAN AND CHILD—
HER RESCUERS HUNG FOR FORMER MURDERS—A LETTER AN-
NOUNCING MY SAFE ARRIVAL AT FORT SULLY.

IMMEDIATELY after Mr. Kelly reached Deer Creek, at the time of our capture, he telegraphed to Fort Laramie of the outbreak of the Indians, and the capture of his wife.

Colonel Collins, of the Eleventh Ohio Cavalry, commandant of the military district, ordered two companies, under Captain Shuman and Captain Marshall, two brave and daring men, to pursue and rescue me, and chastise the savages in case of resistance.

But the distance of one hundred miles lay between these forts, and they only arrived on their way too late for rescue. They continued their march, however, and after an absence of three days returned unsuccessful.

Sad to relate, a young and daring officer, Lieutenant Brown, of the Eleventh Ohio Volunteers, fell a victim to savage cruelty in my behalf, for with a view of prospecting the neighborhood, he, with Mr. Kelly, left the main body with a small squad of men in quest of the Indians.

Coming suddenly upon a band of warriors, in their encampment, the brave Lieutenant indiscreetly ordered an attack, but the men, seeing the futility of opposing such numbers, fled, and left Mr. Kelly and the officer.

Becoming conscious of his dangerous situation, he feigned friendship, addressing them in the usual way, "How koda?" which means, How do you do, friend?

But they were not to be deceived, and sent an arrow, causing him to fall from his horse, and the effects of which caused his death a few hours afterward.

He was immediately reported dead, and with all the speed the men could command they pursued his murderers; but the fresher horses of the savages carried them off beyond their reach, and the soldiers were compelled to return in disappointment.

Brave young man! the ardent friend of Mr. Kelly, and the husband and father of an affectionate wife and child, stricken down in his early manhood, we would humbly lay the wreath of "immortelles" upon thy lonely grave.

After several expeditions in like manner which proved unsuccessful, Mr. Kelly offered a reward of nineteen horses, the money value of which was deposited with the commander of Fort Laramie, and it was circulated through all the Indian villages, that upon my safe delivery the reward would be paid.

Every effort possible was made by my husband and his brothers to procure my rescue or ransom. No money or efforts were spared, and the long days of agonizing suspense to them were worse than death.

The reward which had been offered for my ransom was the means of rescuing another white woman, a Mrs. Ewbanks, and her child, held by the Indians.

The Indian Two-Face and his son, having a desire to enhance their fortunes, paid a few small sums to the other Indians who claimed her, and, taking her with them, set out for Fort Laramie.

When they arrived within a few miles of the fort, the prisoners were left with the son and some others, while Two-Face preceded them to arrange the terms of sale.

The commander agreed to the price, and on the following day Mrs. Ewbanks and her child were brought in—the Indians thinking it made no difference which white woman it was. This was several months after my capture.

Instead of paying the price, the commandant seized and confined them in the guard-house, to await trial for the murder of the ranche-men and the stealing of women and children. The testimony of Mrs. Ewbanks was proof sufficient. They confessed their crimes, and were executed in May following.

In crossing the North Platte River, five miles below the fort, Mrs. Ewbanks had suffered intensely, her child being bound to her back, and she holding on to a log bound by a rope fastened to the saddle of the Indian's horse.

The chief passed over easily, but mother and child were nearly frozen to death by clinging and struggling among masses of broken ice, and protected only by a thin, light garment.

Mr. Kelly sent deputations of Indians with horses, to the Indian villages, with letters to me, which were never delivered. They were not true to their trust, but would come to see me without giving me the messages, then return with the declaration that I could not be found.

He would furnish a complete outfit for an Indian, costing about four hundred dollars, and send him to find me; but the Indian cared only for the money; he would never return.

Having despaired of accomplishing any thing further toward my rescue at Fort Laramie, he left for Leavenworth, to obtain help from citizens there, to get permission of the commander of the division to raise an independent company for my release.

There he met with his brother, General Kelly, who had just returned from the South, and had received a letter from me, acquainting him with my freedom.

Mr. Kelly would not at first be convinced, but, after

being shown the letter, he said, "Yes, I know that is Fanny's writing, but it can not be possible;" and by daylight he was on his way to Dakota.

Who can tell his varied emotions, during that long and wearisome journey, when, at the end, hope held out to him the cup of joy which, after the long suffering of months, he was about to drink. Let only those judge who have been separated from the dearest on earth, and whose fate was involved in mysterious silence, more painful than if the pallid face rested beneath the coffin-lid.

CHAPTER XXV.

SUPPER IN HONOR OF OUR RE-UNION—DEPARTURE FROM FORT SULLY
—INCIDENTS BY THE WAY—ARRIVAL AT GENEVA—MOTHER AND
CHILD—A HAPPY MEETING.

FORT SULLY was garrisoned by three companies of
the Sixth Iowa Cavalry, and I should be recreant to
every sense of justice did I not more particularly express my gratitude to them all—officers and men—for
the delicate, more than brotherly, kindness shown me
during my stay of two months among them.

They had fought gallantly during that summer, and
punished severely the Indians who held me captive;
and though my sufferings at the time were increased
tenfold thereby, I believe the destitute condition of the
Indians had much to do with my final restoration to
freedom. Had there been plenty of food in the Indian villages, none would have gone to Fort Sully to
make a treaty.

On each of the two evenings we remained at the
fort after my husband's arrival, we were honored with
a "feast," in marked contrast with those I had attended while with the savages. Stewed oysters rel-

ished better than stewed dog, and the abundance of other good things, with the happy-looking, kind, sympathetic faces of my own people around the board, filled me with a feeling of almost heavenly content.

Mr. Harry Chatterton presided at the first, and, in a feeling manner, expressed the delight and satisfaction his comrades and himself experienced in this hour of our re-union:

"Sweet is this dream—divinely sweet—
 No dream! no fancy! that you meet;
 Tho' silent grief has shadowed o'er
 To crush your love—it had no power—
 Tho' long divided, you 've met once more
 To tell your toils and troubles o'er;
 Renew the pledge of other days,
 And walk in sweet and pleasant ways

"May the good Father of mercies ever protect and bless you; make the sun of happiness to brightly shine upon you, and may it never again be dimmed by stern misfortune! is the earnest and heartfelt wish of every person in this fort to-day."

With deep emotion these words were spoken, and we felt convinced they were from the innermost depths of the heart.

How many affectionate, generous natures are among us, whom we can never appreciate until some heavy cloud drops down upon us, and they, with their cheerful words and kind acts, assist us to rise, and in hours of joy they are ready to grasp us by the hand, and welcome us to happiness?

Anxious for a re-union with our friends, and to be once more with my dear mother, we bade farewell to those who had shown us so much kindness and attention, and commenced our journey at daylight, to prevent the Indians, many of whom remained about the fort, knowing of my departure, as I was in constant dread of recapture.

Fort Sully is on the Missouri River, three hundred miles from Sioux City, by land, which distance we traveled in an ambulance. At all the military posts, stations, and towns through which we passed, all—military and civilians—seemed to vie with each other in kindness and attention. Those living in frontier towns know what the nature of the Indian is, and could most heartily sympathize with one who had suffered from captivity among them.

At Yankton I received particularly kind attention from Mrs. Ash, of the Ash Hotel, who also gave me the information, elsewhere written, of the fate of Mrs. Dooley and Mrs. Wright. Here, also, I met a number of the Sixth Iowa Cavalry, to which gallant regiment I was under so great obligation. Dr. Bardwell, a surgeon of that regiment, who was at Fort Sully at the time the Blackfeet came in to make a treaty, and were sent off after me, and who, I had previously been informed, was active in measures tending to my release, was stationed at Yankton, and manifested the kindness of his heart in many ways.

At Sioux City, Council Bluffs, and St. Joe, crowds of visitors flocked to see the white woman who had been a captive with the Indians; and I was compelled to answer many questions. From St. Joe, we made all haste for Leavenworth, Kansas, where I was received by friends and relatives as one risen from the dead.

At last we reached our old home in Geneva; the home from which we had departed but a few months before, lured to new fields by the brightest hopes of future prosperity. Alas! what disappointments had fallen to our lot! But soon I was clasped in my dear mother's arms, and all my sorrows were swallowed up in the joy of that re-union.

On the morning of our departure for the plains, she said (while tears of sorrow filled her eyes) that she felt as though it was our final farewell. Her fears were agonizing in my behalf. She seemed to have a presentiment of evil—a dark, portentous cloud hung over my head, she felt, that would burst upon me, and scatter dismay and grief—which too well was realized in the days that followed.

I endeavored to cheer her with hope, and smilingly assured her that, as soon as the Pacific Railroad was completed, I should visit my home and her; and,

though many miles might separate us, we still would
be one in heart; and the facilities for traveling were
becoming so easy and rapid, we could not be separated
for any great length of time. But her sad heart refused to be comforted. A mother's unchanging love—
stronger than death, faithful under every circumstance,
and clinging with tenacity to the child of her affection,
could not part with me without a pang of anguish,
which was increased tenfold when the news of my
capture reached her.

Gradually she sank under this heavy affliction;
health rapidly gave way, and for three long months
she lay helpless, moaning and bewailing the loss of
her children ; for, scarcely had she aroused from the
terrible stupor and grief which the news of my
brother's death from poison, while a soldier in the
Union army, had plunged her, when this new and
awful sorrow came like a whirlwind upon her fainting
spirit.

But God is good. In his great mercy he spared us
both, to meet once more, and a letter from my hand,
telling her of my safety, reached her in due time; and
in each other's fond embrace we were once more
folded.

Oh! happy hour! Methinks the angels smiled in
their celestial abodes when they witnessed that dear
mother's joy.

The reader naturally supposes that here my narrative ought to end; that, restored to husband, mother, and friends, my season of sorrow must be over. But not so. Other trials were in store for me, and, even fortified as I was by past tribulation, I sank almost despairingly under their affliction. Nor was I yet done with the Indians.

Anxious to again establish a home, we left Geneva, went to Shawneetown, where we prospered; but better prospects offering farther west, we went to Ellsworth, a new town just staked out on the western line of Kansas. I was the first woman who located there. We lived in our wagon for a time, then built a hotel, and were prospering, when fears of the Indians again harassed us.

The troops at Fort Harker, four miles east of Ellsworth, had been out, under General Hancock, in pursuit of the Indians, to punish them for murders and depredations committed along the line of the Pacific Railroad, and coming upon an Indian camp, destroyed it, inflicting a severe chastisement. This we knew would so exasperate the Indians as to render the situation of the exposed settlements one of great danger; and after my experience, a terrible dread of again falling into their hands intensified my apprehensions for our safety.

The scouts, Jack Harvey and "Wild Bill," were constantly on the lookout, and eagerly would we look toward the hills for any one who could give us news, and gather around them, when they came from the front, with anxious faces and listening ears.

Meantime the population of Ellsworth had rapidly increased, and military companies were formed for protection. Thus we lived in a continual state of alarm, until at last one night the signal was given that the Indians were approaching, when every man flew to his post, and the women and children fled to the places of refuge that had been prepared for them, an iron-clad house and a "dug-out," or place under ground. I fled to the latter place, where about fifty altogether had congregated, and among them were three young men who were the sole survivors of a large family—father, mother, and two sisters—murdered and horribly mutilated in the Minnesota massacres.

The Indians were repulsed, but they continued to harass us and threaten the town, so that it became necessary to apply for military protection. Accordingly, a number of colored troops were sent there, which imparted a feeling of security.

But Ellsworth was doomed to a more terrible scourge, if possible, than the Indians had threatened to be. The troops were recently from the South. Soon after their arrival among us, the cholera broke out among them, and, spreading among the citizens, created a terrible panic. The pestilence was most destructive, sweeping before it old and young, and of all classes.

My husband fell a victim to the disease.

On the 28th day of July, 1867, a violent attack of this terrible disease carried him off, and, in the midst of peril and cares, I was left a mourning, desolate widow.

Being in delicate health, I was forced to flee to the East, and stopped at St. George, where one week after my little one was ushered into this world of sorrow.

The people were panic-stricken in relation to the cholera, and when I went there, they were afraid to receive me into their homes, consequently I repaired to a small cabin in the outskirts of the town, and my adopted son and myself remained there alone for several days.

A young lady, Miss Baker, called on me in great sympathy, saying she was not afraid of cholera, and would stay with me until after my confinement.

I was very thankful for her kindness, and after the fear was over with the people, every attention that humanity could suggest was given me; but, alas! my heart was at home, and so deep were my yearnings, the physician declared it impossible for me to recover until I did go home.

The events that had transpired seemed like a fearful dream.

The physician who attended me went to Ellsworth to see if it was prudent for me to go, sending a letter immediately after, bidding me come, as the cholera had disappeared.

Oh! how changed was that home! The voice that

had ever been as low, sweet music to my ear was hushed forever; the eye that had always met mine with smiling fondness was closed to light and me, and the hand so often grasped in tender love was palsied in death! Mr. Kelly, the noble, true, and devoted husband, my loved companion, the father of my innocent child, was gone. Oh! how sad that word! My heart was overwhelmed with grief, and that did its work, for it prostrated me on a bed of illness nigh unto death.

Dr. McKennon very faithfully attended me during my illness, and as I was recovering, he was seized by severe sickness himself, which proved fatal.

He was anxious to see me before he died, and desired assistance that he might be taken down stairs for the purpose.

His attendants allowed him to do so, but he fainted in the attempt, and was laid on the floor until he recovered, then raised and placed on the sofa.

I was then led into the room, and, seating myself beside him, he grasped my hand, exclaiming: "My friend, do not leave me. I have a brother in New York"—but his lips soon stiffened in death, and he was unable to utter more.

It was a severe shock to my nervous system, already prostrated by trouble and illness, and I greatly missed his attention and care.

No relative, or friend, was near to lay his weary

head upon the pillow; but we laid him to rest in the burial ground of Ellsworth with sad hearts and great emotion.

In the spring I went to the end of the road further west, with an excursion party, to a place called Sheridan. On our return we stopped at Fort Hays, where I met two Indians who recognized me, and I also knew them. We conversed together. I learned they had a camp in the vicinity, and they were skulking around, reconnoitering. They were well treated here and very liberally dealt with. They inquired where I lived; I told them way off, near to the rising sun.

The next morning, when the train left town, the band, riding on horseback, jumped the ditch, and looked into the windows of the cars, hoping to see me.

They told the people that I belonged to them, and they would take my papoose and me way off to their own country; we were their property, and must go with them.

It was supposed that if I had been in the cars the Indians would have attempted to take the train.

CHAPTER XXVI.

ELIZABETH BLACKWELL—MORMON HOME—A BRUTAL FATHER—THE
MOTHER AND DAUGHTERS FLEE TO THE MOUNTAINS—DEATH OF
THE MOTHER AND SISTERS FROM EXPOSURE—ELIZABETH SAVED
BY AN INDIAN—A WHITE WOMAN TORTURED—RESCUED CHILDREN
THE DOXX FAMILY—CAPTURE OF MRS. BLYNN—

SOME few weeks after the events just related, I received a note from a stranger, requesting me to call
on her at the dwelling of a hunter, where she was
stopping. Her name was Elizabeth Blackwell, and
emigrated with her parents from England, who became
proselytes of the ruling prophet of Salt Lake City,
where they remained until Elizabeth's father took another wife. This created trouble; words ensued, soon
followed by blows, and Elizabeth, in endeavoring to
protect her mother, was struck by her brute of a father
with a knife, and one of her eyes destroyed.

Being discouraged and broken-hearted, the wretched
mother and daughters (for Elizabeth had two sisters)
resolved to escape. They wandered away among the
mountains, and, having no place of shelter, all perished
with the cold, except Elizabeth, who was found by the

Indians, nearly frozen to death. They lifted her up and carried her to camp, where they gave her every attention requisite for restoration.

She remained with the Indians until she was able to go east, where she underwent the severe operation of having both legs amputated above the knee.

The treatment received from the Indians so attached her to them that she prefers to live a forest life, and when she gave me her narrative, she was on her way from the States to her Indian home.

Her father soon wearied of his Mormon wife, and escaped to the Rocky Mountains, where he became a noted higwayman. Hearing of Elizabeth's residence among the Indians, he visited her, and gave her a large sum of money. The fate of his family had great effect on him, and remorse drove him to desperation.

The husband of Elizabeth took his second wife and Elizabeth's child from Salt Lake to Cincinnati, where they now live.

She was twenty-six years old when I saw and conversed with her, a lady of intelligence, and once possessed more than ordinary beauty.

She had just received the news of her father's death. He was killed near Fort Dodge, Kansas.

Elizabeth related to me many acts of cruelty she had witnessed among the savages, one of which was to the following effect:

A woman was brought into the camp on horseback,

who had been captured from a train, and an Indian who was attempting to lift her from the horse, was shot in the act, by her own hand. This so enraged the savages that they cut her body in gashes, filled them with powder, and then set fire to it.

The sight of the woman's sufferings was too much for Elizabeth to endure, and she begged the savages to put an end to the victim at once, which accordingly was done.

But although Elizabeth saw many heartless acts— many terrible scenes—still she had a kindly feeling toward the Indians, for they saved her from a horrible death by starvation and exposure, and had been very tender with her. She was somewhat embittered toward the white people, on account of her sufferings, and treatment.

A short time after, General Sully invited me to Fort Harker, to see two white captive children, a girl of fourteen and a boy of six. They had been captured two years before, and the account of their treatment given me by the girl, was any thing but favorable. The boy was as wild as a deer.

A Sioux woman at Fort Harker had taken these children into her own family and cared for them as a mother. She was the daughter of a white man, was born at Fort Laramie, and had married an interpreter by the name of Bradley. She was quite intelligent, having been educated by her husband.

In January, 1868, two other children were captured in the State of Texas by the Kiowa Indians. They were girls, aged five and three years. Their parents and all the known relatives had been murdered, and the children had been recently recovered from the Indians, and were in the care of J. H. Leavenworth, United States Indian Agent. Having no knowledge of their parentage, they were named Helen and Heloise Lincoln.

Another interesting family was taken from Texas by the Indians, their beautiful home destroyed, and all killed with the exception of the mother and three daughters.

Their name was Boxx. The ages of the children were respectively eighteen, fourteen, and ten, and they were allowed to be together for a time, but afterward were separated.

They experienced great cruelties. The youngest was compelled to stand on a bed of live coals, in order to torture the mother and sisters.

Lieutenant Hesselberger, the noble and brave officer, whose name will live forever in the hearts of the captives he rescued, heard of this family, and, with a party of his brave men, went immediately to the Indian village, and offered a reward for the captives, which at first was declined, but he at length succeeded in purchasing the mother and one girl; he afterward procured the release of the others.

Lieutenant Hesselberger braved death in so doing, and his only reward is the undying gratitude of those who owe their lives to his self-sacrificing, humane devotion and courage.

In the fall of 1868, the Indians commenced depredations on the frontier of Kansas, and after many serious outbreaks, destroying homes and murdering settlers, the Governor issued a call for volunteers to assist General Sheridan in protecting the settlers and punishing the Indians. Among those who volunteered was my youngest brother, and many of my old schoolmates and friends from Geneva, who related to me the following incidents, which are fully substantiated by General Sheridan and others.

Mrs. Morgan, an accomplished and beautiful bride, and Miss White, an educated young lady, were both taken from their homes by the Indians. They were living on the Republican River.

During their captivity they suffered much from the inclemency of the weather, and it was March before they were released by General Sheridan.

The troops, the Kansas boys, were all winter among the mountains, endeavoring to protect the frontier.

They suffered great privation, being obliged sometimes to live on the meat of mules, and often needing food. All honor to these self-sacrificing men, who braved the cold and hunger of the mountains to protect the settlers on the frontier.

A Mrs. Blynn, whose maiden name was Harrington, of Franklin County, Kansas, who was married at the age of nineteen, and started with her young husband for the Pacific coast, was taken prisoner by the Indians and suffered terrible brutality.

About that time the savages had become troublesome on the plains, attacking every wagon-train, killing men and capturing women. But the train in which Mr. Blynn and his wife traveled was supposed to be very strong, and able to repel any attack made upon them, should there be any such trouble.

Mrs. Blynn had a presentiment of evil—of the fate of their unfortunate company, and her own dark impending destiny, in a dream, the realization of which proved too true.

When she related her dream to her husband, he tried to laugh away her superstitious fears, and prevent its impression on her mind.

It was not many days after that a large number of warriors of the Sioux tribe were seen in the distance, and the people of the train arranged themselves in a shape for attack.

The Indians, seeing this preparation, and, fearing a powerful resistance, fired a few shots, and, with yells of rage and disappointment, went off.

Within the succeeding days the travelers saw Indians, but they did not come near enough to make trouble.

Confident of no disturbance or hinderance to their journey, the happy emigrants journeyed on fearless (comparatively) of the red skins, and boasting of their power.

But the evil hour at last approached. When the column had reached Sand Creek, and was in the act of crossing, suddenly the wild yells of Indians fell upon their ears, and soon a band of Cheyennes charged down upon them.

Two wagons had already got into the stream, and, instead of hastening the others across, and thus putting the creek between themselves and their pursuers, the whites drove the two back out of the water, and, entangled in the others, threw every thing in confusion. This confusion is just what the Indians like, and they began whooping, shouting, and firing furiously, in order to cause a stampede of the live-stock.

In five minutes all was accomplished; all the animals, except those well fastened to the wagons, were dashing over the prairie. The Indians then circled around and fired a volley of bullets and arrows. Mr. Blynn was killed at the second fire, while standing before the wagon in which were his wife and child.

"God help them!" was all he said, as, firing his rifle at the Indians for the last time, he sank down dead.

The men returned the fire for awhile, then fled, leaving their wounded, all their wagons, and the women and children in the hands of the relentless victors.

Santana, who led the band, sprang in first, followed by his braves, whom he ordered to let the cowardly pale faces run away without pursuit.

The dead and wounded were scalped, and the women and children taken captive.   All were treated with brutal conduct; and, having secured all the plunder they could, the savages set fire to every wagon, and, with the horses they had taken from the train, set out in the direction of their villages.

Mrs. Blynn's child, Willie, two years old, cried very much, which so enraged Santana that he seized him by the heels, and was ready to dash out his brains, but the poor mother, in her agony, sprang forward, caught the child, and fought so bravely with the infuriated murderer, that he laughed, and told her to keep it; for he feared she would fret if he killed it.

Mounted on a pony, her child in her arms, she endeavored to please her savage captor by appearing satisfied, dwelling on the hope that some event would occur, whereby she might be rescued and restored to her friends.   It was for her darling child that she endeavored to keep up her heart and resolve to live.

When they arrived at Santana's village, Mrs. Blynn was left alone of all the seven who were taken.   Group after group dropped away from the main body, taking with them the women whom they had prisoners.

Her hardships soon commenced. For a day or two she was fed sufficiently; but afterward all that she had to eat she got from the squaws in the same lodge with her; and, as they were jealous of her, they often refused to give her any thing, either for herself or Willie.

An Indian girl, in revenge for an injury done her by Santana, the murder of her best friend, became a spy for General Sheridan, and endeavored by every means in her power to rescue Mrs. Blynn from the grasp of these savages; but her efforts were unsuccessful. She was a true friend to the unfortunate lady, giving her food, and endeavoring to cheer her with the promise of rescue and safe deliverance.

The squaws abused her shamefully in the absence of Santana, burning her with sharp sticks and splinters of resinous wood, and inflicting the most excruciating tortures upon her. Her face, breasts, and limbs were one mass of wounds. Her precious little one was taken by the hair of the head and punished with a stick before her helpless gaze.

Mrs. Blynn, the captive, previous to this torture, had written a letter to the general commanding the department, whoever he might be, and sent it by the Indian girl.

We insert a copy of this letter, which is sufficient to draw tears from the eye of any one who may read it.

"Kiowah Village, on the Washita River. }
Saturday, *November* 7, 1868. }

" Kind Friend :

"Whoever you may be, if you will only buy us from the Indians with ponies or any thing, and let me come and stay with you until I can get word to my friends, they will pay you well; and I will work for you also, and do all I can for you.

"If it is not too far to this village, and you are not afraid to come, I pray you will try.

"The Indians tell me, as near as I can understand, they expect traders to come, to whom they will sell us. Can you find out by the bearer, and let me know if they are white men? If they are Mexicans, I am afraid they will sell us into slavery in Mexico.

"If you can do nothing for me, write, for God's sake! to W. T. Harrington, Ottawa, Franklin County, Kansas—my father. Tell him we are with the Kiowahs, or Cheyennes; and they say when the white men make peace we can go home.

"Tell him to write to the Governor of Kansas about it, and for them to make peace. Send this to him, please.

"We were taken on October 9th, on the Arkansas, below Fort Lyon. My name is Mrs. Clara Blynn. My little boy, Willie Blynn, is two years old.

"Do all you can for me. Write to the Peace Commissioners to make peace this fall. For our sake do all you can, and God will bless you for it!

"If you can let me hear from you, let me know what you think about it. Write to my father. Send him this. Good-by!

"MRS. R. F. BLYNN.

"P. S.—I am as well as can be expected, but my baby, my darling, darling little Willie, is very weak. O, God! help him! Save him, kind friend, even if you can not save me. Again, good-by."

Mrs. Blynn passed her time in drudgery, hoping against hope up to the morning of the battle, when General Sheridan's gallant soldiers, under the command of General Custer, came charging with loud huzzahs upon the village.

Black Kettle's camp was the first attacked, though all the village was, of course, aroused.

The heart of Mrs. Blynn must have beat wildly, mingling with hope and dread, when she heard the noise and firing, and saw the United States soldiers charging upon her captors.

Springing forward, she exclaimed: "Willie, Willie, saved at last!" but the words were scarce on her lips, ere the tomahawk of the revengeful Santana was buried in her brain; and in another instant little Willie was in the grasp of the monster, and his head dashed against a tree; then, lifeless, he was thrown upon the dying mother's breast, whose arms instinctively closed around the dead baby boy, as though she would protect him to the last moment of her life.

General Sheridan and his staff, in searching for the bodies of Major Elliott and his comrades, found these among the white soldiers, and they were tenderly carried to Fort Cobb, where, in a grave outside the stockade, mother and child lie sleeping peacefully, their once bruised spirits having joined the loved husband and father in the land where captivity is unknown.

Surely, if heaven is gained by the sorrows of earth, this little family will enjoy the brightest scenes of the celestial world.

CHAPTER XXVII.

MOVE TO WYOMING—FALSE FRIENDS—THE MANUSCRIPT OF MY NAR-
RATIVE TAKEN BY ANOTHER PARTY AND PUBLISHED — I GO TO
WASHINGTON.

MR. KELLY's sudden death, my own sickness, and
the scourge of cholera, all coming at one time, proved
disastrous to me in a pecuniary way. I was defrauded
in every way, even to the robbing of my husband's
body of the sum of five hundred dollars the day of his
death. However, I finally disposed of the remnant
of property left, and started for Wyoming, where lived
the only persons beside myself who survived the attack
on our train. They had prospered, and in a spirit of
kindness, as I then thought, invited and prevailed on
me to share their home.

It proved a most disastrous move for me. My
leisure hours, since my release from captivity, had
been devoted to preparing for publication, in book
form, a narrative of my experience and adventures
among the Indians, and it was completed. The
manuscript was surreptitiously taken, and a gar-
bled, imperfect account of my captivity issued as the
experience of my false friend, who, by the aid of an

Indian, escaped after a durance of only one day and night.

I remained in Wyoming one year, then started for Washington, resolved to present a claim to the Government for losses sustained at the hands of the Indians. I knew what difficulties beset my path, but duty to my child urged me on, and I was not without some hope of success.

After learning of my captivity through Captain Fisk, President Lincoln had issued orders to the different military commanders that my freedom from the Indians must be purchased at any price; and my sad story was well known to the then existing authorities when I arrived in Washington.

President Grant, learning through a friend from Colorado of my presence, sent for me, and assured me of his warmest sympathy. He was cognizant of what had already transpired relative to me, and told me the papers were on file in the War Department, in charge of General Sherman.

In presenting my claim, many difficulties had to be encountered; but members of Congress, realizing that some compensation was due me, and understanding the delay that would result from a direct application to the Indian Bureau, introduced a bill appropriating to me five thousand dollars for valuable services rendered the Government in saving Captain Fisk's train from destruction, and by timely warning saving Fort Sully from pillage, and its garrison from being massacred. This was done without my having any knowledge of it until after the bill had passed both houses of Congress and become a law.

During my stay in Washington, Red Cloud, and a delegation of chiefs and head warriors from the different tribes of the Dakota or Sioux nation, arrived. They all recognized me as once having been with their people, and seemed quite rejoiced at the meeting.

Some of the good Christian people of the city extended to the Indians, through me, an invitation to attend church one Sabbath, which I made known to Red Cloud, telling him of the great organ, the fine music they would hear, and of the desire the good people had to benefit their souls.

Red Cloud replied with dignity that he did not have to go to the big house to talk to the Great Spirit; he could sit in his tipi or room, and the Great Spirit would listen. The Great Spirit was not where the big music was. No, he would not go.

None of the Indians accepted the invitation; but some of the squaws went, escorted to the church in elegant carriages; but they soon left in disgust. The dazzling display of fine dresses, the beautiful church, and the "big music"—none of these had interest for them, if unaccompanied by a feast.

I attended several of the councils held with the Indians.   At one of them, Red Cloud addressed Secretary Cox and Commissioner Parker in a lengthy speech on the subject of his grievances, in which he referred to me as follows.   Pointing me out to the Secretary and Commissioner, he said :

"Look at that woman; she was captured by Silver Horn's party.   I wish you to pay her what her captors owe her.   I am a man true to what I say, and want to keep my promise.   I speak for all my nation.   The Indians robbed that lady there, and through your influence I want her to be paid out of the first money due us."   Placing his finger first upon the breast of the Secretary and then of the Commissioner, as if to add emphasis to what he was about to say, he added, "Pay her out of our money ; do not give the money into any but her own hands; then the right one will get it."

In one of my interviews with the chiefs, Red Cloud, Spotted Tail, and others desired me to get up a paper setting forth my claims against their people, and they would sign it.   I accordingly made out a bill of items and presented it to them, with my affidavit, and a statement setting forth the circumstances of capture and robbery, which was fully explained to them by their interpreter.

This document the chiefs representing the different bands signed readily.   It is inserted elsewhere, with other documents corroborative of the truth of this narrative. It is also signed by another delegation of chiefs I met in New York.

With this last interview with the delegation of Indians I met in New York ends, I trust forever, my experience with Indians. The preparation of the manuscript for this plain, simple narrative of facts in my experience, has not been without its pangs. It has seemed, while writing it, as if with the narration of each incident, I was living over again the fearful life I led while a captive; and often have I laid aside the pen to get rid of the feelings which possessed me. But my task is completed; and with the ending of this chapter, I hope to lay aside forever all regretful remembrances of my captivity, and, looking only at the silvery lining to be found in every cloud, enjoy the happiness which every one may find in child-like trust in Him who ordereth all things well.

CHAPTER XXVIII.

GENERAL SULLY'S EXPEDITION.

DURING the summer of 1864, and while I was a prisoner with the Indians, an expedition, composed of Iowa and Minnesota volunteers, with a few independent companies of Nebraska and Dakota men, with one company of friendly Indians of various tribes, started from Fort Sully, in Dakota, with the double purpose, under instructions from the War Department, of escorting a large emigrant train safely through the Indian country on their way to Idaho, and, if possible, to inflict such punishment on the hostile bands they might meet as would make them willing to sue for peace.

The expedition was commanded by General Alfred Sully, of the United States Army, a brave, skillful officer, and veteran Indian fighter, having spent the best part of twenty-five years' service on the frontier. He was a captain of infantry under General Harney, in his memorable campaign of 1857, and was present at the battle of Ash Hollow, where Harney surprised a large band of Indians, with their families, who were slaughtered indiscriminately, inflicting such punishment as made the name of General Harney a terror to the Indians, and, at the same time, brought upon his head the execration of thin-skinned philanthropists, who thought savages—the "noble red men" of their imagination—should be conquered only by a sugar-plum and rose-water policy.

For many interesting particulars of this expedition, and its bearing upon some of the incidents of my captivity and final ransom, I am indebted to the correspondence of one who was a member of the expedition, written to his family during its progress.

The first day's march carries the command to the Cheyenne River, where the topographical engineer, to whom I have referred, was killed. His fate was sad, indeed. An officer in the regular army, he served with distinction in the South during the rebellion, participating in over fifty battles, and passing through all without a wound. He was captured by the rebels, paroled, and sent to join General Sully's expedition, to make a topographical survey of the country.

Having faced danger on many a well-contested field, he held the Indian in utter contempt, and roamed the country along the line of march with reckless indifference to danger.

A short time before reaching the place where the command intended to go into camp, Captain Fielner started in advance, accompanied by only one man, a half-breed. Reaching the river, they dismounted, and were about fastening their horses to graze near a grove of wild plum-trees, when two Indians stepped out, and one of them shot Captain Fielner, the ball from his rifle passing through both arms and the breast. The advance guard arriving soon after, word was sent back to General Sully, who ordered the company of Dakota Cavalry to deploy and occupy so much of the country as to make it impossible for the Indians to escape. This was done, and, closing toward a center, the two savages were found in a " buffalo wallow," a depression in the ground made by the buffalos, and forming a very good rifle-pit. Being addressed in their own language, they refused to surrender, and were shot. General Sully afterward had their heads cut off; and when the command left camp next morning, they graced two pointed stakes on the bank of the river, placed there as a warning to all straggling Indians.

The feeling manifested by General Sully on the occasion of Captain Fielner's death was intense. A brave officer, a scientific scholar, and a gentleman of rare social qualities, he had won upon the kindlier feelings of his associates in rank, and was respected by all. His untimely death was sincerely mourned by the whole command.

Death by the hand of the enemy had seldom touched that little army—so seldom, that when a companion failed to answer at roll-call, his absence was felt. The only other officer killed during the three years of General Sully's operations against the Indians was Lieutenant Thomas K. Leavitt, of Company B, Sixth Iowa Cavalry. At the battle of Whitestone Hill, in September, 1863, after the Indians had been utterly routed, Lieutenant Leavitt went through their deserted camp on foot, his horse having been shot under him; and, approaching a buffalo robe, raised it with the point of his saber, revealing an Indian and squaw, who sprang upon him so suddenly that he had no opportunity to defend himself, and, with their knives, stabbed him in several places. Darkness came on, and, separated from his companions, stripped of his clothing, and wounded mortally, he was all night exposed to bitter cold. Despite his wounds, he crawled over the ground fully a half mile, was found next morning, and conveyed to camp, where he died soon after. A young man of superior education, of a wealthy family, he relinquished a lucrative position in a bank, and enlisted as a private, but was soon promoted to a lieutenancy; and, at the time of his death, was acting Adjutant-General on General Sully's staff.

The emigrant train to be escorted by General Sully's command came across from Minnesota, and were met at a point on the Missouri River about four hundred miles above Sioux City. Here the whole party crossed to the west bank of the Missouri, where they went into camp, and remained long enough to recruit their jaded animals, preparatory to a long and fatiguing march into an almost unknown wilderness, jealously guarded by a savage foe.

During this halt, Fort Rice, now one of the most important fortifications on the Missouri River, was built, and, when the march was resumed, a considerable portion of the command was left to garrison it.

Here, also, General Sully learned that all the tribes of the Sioux nation had congregated in the vicinity of Knife River, determined to resist his passage through their country, and confident that superior numbers would enable them to annihilate the whole expedition, and gain a rich booty in horses and goods, to say nothing of the hundreds of scalp-locks they hoped to win as trophies of their prowess.

About the middle of July the expedition took up its march westward, and after a few days reached Heart River. Meantime, information had been received, from Indians employed as scouts, that the enemy had gathered in strong force at a place called Ta-ka-a-ku-ta, or Deer Woods, about eighty miles to the north-west, and that distance out of the proposed route of the expedition. Accordingly, General Sully ordered the emigrant train and heavy army wagons corralled, rifle-pits were dug, and, as the emigrants were generally well armed, it was deemed necessary to leave only a small force of cavalry to protect them in case of attack.

Putting the balance of the command in light marching order, leaving behind tents and all other articles not absolutely necessary, the little band of determined men started for the camp of the enemy. Although the Indians were aware of the contemplated attack, such was the celerity of General Sully's movements, he came within sight of their camp at least twenty-four hours sooner than they thought it possible the distance could be accomplished, taking the Indians by surprise, they not having time, as is their custom, to remove their property and women and children beyond the reach of danger.

I was present with this body of Indians when the white soldiers—my countrymen—came in sight. Alternating between hope and fear, my feelings can be better imagined than described. I hoped for deliverance, yet feared disaster and death to that little army.

At 1 o'clock in the afternoon the fight commenced, and raged, with great fury, until night closed on the scene of conflict, leaving the whites masters of the field and in possession of the Indian camp.

Early in the day, I, with the women and children and old men, and such property as could be gathered in our hasty flight, was sent off so as to be out of the way, not to impede the flight of the Indians in case of defeat.

This was a terrible blow to the Indians. About eight thousand of them were gathered there, and their village, with all their property (except their horses and dogs), including all the stores of provisions they had gathered for the winter, were lost. Without shelter, without food, driven into a barren, desolate region, devoid of game, death from starvation seemed inevitable.

Early next morning pursuit was commenced, but after a march of about five miles was abandoned, as the country beyond was impassable for cavalry. Returning to the scene of the previous day's battle, General Sully spent several hours in destroying the property abandoned by the Indians in their flight. Lodge poles were piled together and fired, and into the flames was cast furs, robes, tents, provisions, and every thing that fell into the hands of the soldiers.

That night the command camped about six miles from, but within sight of, the battle-ground, going into camp early in the afternoon. Picket guards were stationed on the hills, three at a post, and soon after the camp was thrown into commotion by the appearance of one of the guard dashing toward camp, at the full speed of his horse, with Indians in pursuit. His companions, worn out with the arduous service of the preceding three days, had laid down to sleep, and before the one remaining on guard could give the alarm, a body of Indians was close upon them. Discharging his rifle to arouse his companions, he had barely time to reach his horse and escape. The bodies

of the other two were found next day horribly mutilated; and that night, being within sight of the battle-
ground, the firelight revealed the forms of a large body
of savages dancing around the burning ruins of their
own homes.

Returning to Heart River, General Sully took the
emigrants again in charge, and resumed the march
toward Idaho.

Traversing a country diversified and beautiful as the
sun ever shone upon, presenting at every turn pictures
of natural beauty, such as no artist ever represented on
canvas, the expedition at last struck the "Mauvais
Terra," or Bad Lands, a region of the most wildly
desolate country conceivable. No pen of writer, nor
brush of painter, can give the faintest idea of its awful
desolation.

As the command halted upon the confines of this
desert, the mind naturally reverted to political descrip-
tions of the infernal regions reached in other days.

The Bad Lands of Dakota extend from the con-
fluence of the Yellow Stone and Missouri Rivers
toward the south-west, a distance of about one hundred
miles, and are from twenty-five to forty miles in width.
The foot of white man had never trod these wilds
before.

The first day's march into this desert carried the
expedition ten miles only, consuming ten hours of
time, and leaving the forces four miles from, and

within sight of, the camp, they left in the morning. On the 7th of August, the advance guard were attacked in the afternoon by a large party of Indians. After a toilsome march of many days, a valley in the wilderness was reached, presenting an opportunity for rest, and here the first vegetation was found for the famished horses.   In this valley the troops camped; the advance guard were brought back, having suffered some from the attack of the ambushed savages.

Next day commenced one of the most memorable battles ever fought with Indians in the whole experience of the Government.   The whole Dakota nation, including the supposed friendly tribes, was concentrated there, and numbered fully eight thousand warriors. Opposed to them was a mere handful, comparatively, of white men.   But they were led by one skilled in war, and who knew the foe he had to contend against.

For three days the fight raged, and, finally, on the night of the third day, and after a toilsome march of ten days through the "Bad Lands," the command reached a broad, open country, where the savages made a final, desperate stand to drive the invaders back. They were the wild Dakotians, who had seen but little of the white settlements, and had a contemptuous opinion.   But a new lesson was to be learned, and it cost them dearly.   They had seen guns large and small, but the little mountain howitzers, from which shells were sent among them, they could not comprehend, and asked the Indian scouts accompanying the expedition if all the wagons " shot twice." Terrible punishment was inflicted upon the Indians in that three days' fight.

At the close of the second day, the brigade wagon-master reported that he had discovered the tracks of a white woman, and believed the Indians held one captive. This was the first intimation General Sully received of my captivity, and, not having received from the western posts any report of captures by Indians, thought it must be some half-breed woman who wore the foot gear of civilization.

But the sympathetic nature of that brave, noble General was stirred to its depths, when his Indian scouts brought in the report that they had talked with the hostile foe, and they had tauntingly said, " we have a white woman captive."

The Indians were badly whipped, and having accomplished that portion of his mission, General Sully went on with his emigrant train to the Yellow Stone River, and beyond that there were long, toilsome marches, but no battles.

Early in October the command arrived opposite Fort Rice, and went into camp. The tents of the little band of white warriors were hardly pitched before word came that Captain Fisk, with a large party of emigrants and a small escort of soldiers, had been attacked by a large party of Indians; had corralled their train, and could not move, but were on the defensive, and were confident of holding out until relief should come. They were distant about one hundred and eighty miles, and the sympathetic nature of the veteran, while it condemned the action of his junior officer, thrilled with an earnest desire to save the women and children of that apparently doomed train.

A detail of men from each company of the command was made, and Captain Fisk and his train of emigrants rescued from their perilous situation. Here was received proof positive of the fact that a white woman was held captive by the Indians; and while every man would have been willing to risk his life for her rescue, and many applications were made to the General for permission to go out on expeditions for that purpose, he had already adopted such measures as must secure her release.

Friendly Indians who had accompanied the expedition were sent out to visit the various tribes, to assure them of an earnest desire on the part of the whites for peace, and invite them to meet at Fort Sully to make a treaty. The result was that about the latter part of October the vicinity of the fort presented an unusual appearance of animation. Several bands had come in, in anticipation of the big feast that had hitherto preceded all talks. Their disappointment may be imagined when they were told that no talk would be had, nor any feast given, until they brought in the white woman.

Their protestations, that she was not their captive, and that they could not get her from the band who held her, were of no avail, and, at length, Tall Soldier, who was thought to be friendly, called for volunteers to go with him for the white woman. About one hundred Indians responded, and the assurance was given that they would get the captive, if even at the expense of a fight with those they went to take her from.

Weeks of painful suspense passed, and then came a letter from the captive woman, brought by an Indian, in which warning was given of an intent to capture the fort and murder the garrison. The warning was acted upon; and when, on the 12th day of December, a large body of Indians appeared on the bluffs overlooking the fort, that little band of not more than two hundred men was prepared to give them a warm reception should they come with hostile intent. Not only were arms in prime condition, but every heart beat with high resolve.

When the cavalcade drew up in front of the fort, and the captive woman, with about twelve of her immediate savage attendants, had passed through the gates, they were ordered closed, shutting out the main body, and leaving them exposed to a raking fire from the guns in the bastions.

But no attack was made. The Indians seemed to know that the little band of soldiers were prepared, and went quietly into camp, on an island opposite the

fort. Next day a council was held, and the terms of
the captives surrender agreed upon. Three unservice-
able horses, to replace ponies left with the Ogalallas
by the Blackfeet, as a pledge for the captives return;
also, fifty dollars worth of presents, some provisions,
and a promise of a treaty when General Sully should
return. The Indians remained about the fort nearly
two weeks, and during that time efforts were made to
induce the captive woman to leave the fort and visit
them at their lodges, doubtless with the design of
recapturing her. After making the captive some
presents, they bade adieu. Two months later they
returned, apparently very much disappointed when
they found the captive had left for her home. They
were soon again upon the war path.

DEDICATED TO MRS. FANNY KELLY.

BY A SOLDIER.

In early youth, far in the distant west,
With gentle steps the fragrant fields you pressed;
Then joy rebounded in thy youthful heart,
Nor thought of care, or trouble, bore no part.
The morn of life, whose sky seems ever bright,
And distant hills are tinged with crimson light,
When hope, bright hope, by glowing fancies driven,
Fill'd thy young heart with raptured thoughts of heaven.
'T was there, 'neath yonder glorious westernsky,
Where noble forests wave their heads on high,
And gentle zephyrs, filled with rich perfume,
Swept o'er vast prairies in undying bloom;
And there where silvery lakes and rippling streams
Go murmuring through the hills and valleys green,
And birds sing gayly, as they soar along,
In gentle notes, their ever-welcome song.
'T was there was passed thy youthful life away,
And all became a dread reality;
Then woo'd and wedded to the one you loved,
As partner of thy life all else above;
To share thy brightest hopes, or gloomy fears,
Or mingle in thy smiles, or gushing tears;
To be to theera constant bosom friend,
Faithful and true till life's last hours should end:
Those days and years so pleasantly passed by,
No tears of grief—thy bosom knew no sigh;
But, ah! those days, those halcyon days, are past,
Those sunny hours, they were too sweet to last!
For far out o'er the broadest prairie plain,
Onward you pressed a distant home to gain.

Days, even weeks, so pleasantly passed o'er,
That mem'ry brought back those sweet days of yore;
Those days of thy youth for which you did sigh,
But ne'er did ye think that some soon should die.
For days of sadness, those days that come to all,
From the humblest cot to the palace hall,
When gathering darkness cloud the clear, blue sky,
Our brightest prospects all in ruin lie.
While gathering round the camp at close of day,
As the sun shed forth her last but lingering ray,
The war-whoop of the Sioux Indian band
Was heard; "They come," and all surrounded stand.
A moment more, and then around thee lay,
As the dark smoke had cleared itself away,
The lifeless forms of those in horror slain,
And thou, alas! the only one remain.
No bosom friend, no counselor is near,
To sooth thy troubled breast, or quell thy fear.
Those dearest by all earthly ties are fled,
And you, a captive, stand among the dead;
For months in bondage to this savage band,
With none to rescue from his cruel hand,
To rove with them o'er prairies far and wild,
Far from thy husband and thy murdered child.
No star of hope, nor sun's resplendent light,
Sends down one gleam upon this fearful night;
No power to pierce the dark and hidden gloom,
That veils the heart while in this earthly tomb.
But, lo! a change, a wondrous change, to thee!
Once held a captive, but now from bondage free.
The great Jehovah reigns; His arm is strong,
He sets the captive free, though waiteth long,
And turns the darkest hours of midnight gloom,
Into the effulgent brightness of noon.

W. S. V. H.

CERTIFICATE OF INDIAN CHIEFS.

Personally appeared before me, a Notary Public for the District of Columbia, Mrs. Fanny Kelly, who is at this time a citizen of the State of Kansas, and being duly sworn, deposes and says:

That in the year 1864, she started from Geneva, Allen County, Kansas, for the purpose of settling with her husband and family in Montana, and for this purpose she with her husband took all the goods and chattles they had, which are enumerated below, with amount and value.

She further says she is now a widow and has a family to support.

But she was for many months a prisoner, and taken captive by a band of the Sioux Indians, at the time at war with the white people, and with the United States, as follows: On the 12th day of July, 1864, while on the usually traveled road across the plains, and west of Fort Laramie, she, with her husband and family, with several other persons, were attacked by these Indians, and five of the party were killed, while she was taken captive. That the Indians took or destroyed all they had. She was a captive for five months, suffered hardships and taunts, and was finally delivered to the military authorities of the United States in Dakota, at Fort Sully.

That the following is a statement of their goods and effects, including stock, as near as she can remember.

The whole account was made out and placed, as she is informed, in the hands of Dr. Burleigh, late delegate from Dakota, but which she can not find at this time. The amount and the leading items she knows to be as follows:

*   *   *   *   *   *

FANNY KELLY

Subscribed and sworn to before me, this 24th day of February, A. D. 1870.

JAS. H. McKENNEY, Notary Public,
Washington County, D. C.

CITY OF WASHINGTON,   }
  District of Columbia,
     June 9th, 1870.

We, the undersigned, chiefs and head men of the Dakota or Sioux Indians, do hereby acknowledge and certify to the facts set forth in the foregoing affidavit of Mrs. Fanny Kelly, as to her captivity and to the destruction of her property by members of our nation. We acknowledge the justness of her claim against us for the loss of her goods, and desire that the same may be paid her out of any moneys now due our nation, or that may become due us by annuity or by any appropriation made by Congress; and we would respectfully request that the amount as set forth in the foregoing bill be paid to Mrs. Fanny Kelly by the Department, out of any funds that may now or hereafter belong to us.

SPOTTED × TAIL,
  Chief of Brule Sioux.
SWIFT × BEAR,
  Chief of Brule Sioux.
FAST × BEAR,
  Warrior, Brule Sioux.
YELLOW × HAIR,
  Warrior, Brule Sioux.

I certify that I was present when the above statment was signed by said Brule Sioux chiefs and warriors, and that the same was fully explained to them before they subscribed to same by the interpreter.

CHAS. E. GUERU,
Sioux Interpreter.

WASHINGTON, D. C., June 9, 1870.

Witnessed by:
DEWITT C. POOLE,
    Captain U. S. Army, and Agent for Sioux Indians.

RED × CLOUD,
RED × DOG,
ROCKY × BEAR,
LONG × WOLF,
SWORD ×
SETTING × BEAR,
LITTLE × BEAR,
YELLOW ×

I certify that I was present when the above statement was signed by the Ogallala chiefs and warriors, and that the same was fully explained to them before they subscribed to the same by the interpreter.

JOHN RICHARD

Witness:
JUELS COFFEY.

WASHINGTON, D. C., June 11, 1870.

LITTLE × SWAN,
PRETTY × BEAR,
BLACK × TOMAHAWK,
RED × FEATHER.

I certify on honor that I was present when the above statement was signed by the said chiefs and warriors of the Minniconyon and Saus Arcs bands of Sioux Indians, aud that the same was fully explained to them by

BAZEL $\overset{\text{his}}{\times}$ CLEMENS,
mark.
Interpreter.

Witness:

F. D. Curtis.

GEO. M. RANDALL,
Capt. and Brvt. Maj. U. S. A.,
Indian Agent.

NEW YORK, July 14, 1870.

Red Cloud, the Orator Sioux Chief.

CERTIFIED COPIES OF MY CORRESPOND-
ENCE WITH CAPTAIN FISK.

WASHINGTON, D. C., January 13, 1865.

L. THOMAS, Adjutant General, U. S. A.,
             Washington, D. C.

GENERAL :

*   *   *   *   *   *   *

We made our start from Fort Ridgley, where I had received the kindest attentions and important favors from the officers in charge, on the afternoon of the 15th of July.

*   *   *   *   *   *   *

THE TRUCE—A CAPTIVE WHITE WOMAN.

Soon there was a gathering of what appeared to be all the Indians about, on an eminence of prairie one mile away, and in full sight of the camp. There came from the crowd three unarmed warriors toward the train, holding up a white flag which they planted in the ground about seven hundred yards off, and then retired.

This was an unexpected phase to the affair. While we were making extra preparations for war, there came a truce. I sent Mitchell, my brave and efficient officer of the guard, with two Sioux half-bred interpreters to ascertain the meaning of this overture. They found, on reaching the ground, a letter stuck in a stick, and directed to me. Without pausing to converse with the Indians, who were a few rods distant, my assistant returned to camp with the letter. That letter appeared to have been written by a white woman, a captive in the hands of the Indians, and read as follows:

"Makatunke says he will not fight wagons, for they have been fighting two days. They had many killed by the goods they brought into camp. They tell me what to write. I do not understand them. I was taken by them July 12. They say for the soldiers to give forty head of cattle.

"Hehutalunca says he fights not, but they have been fighting. Be kind to them, and try to free me, for mercy's sake.

"I was taken by them July 12.
    (Signed)   "MRS. KELLY."

"Buy me if you can, and you will be satisfied. They have killed many whites. Help me if you can.

"Unkpapas (they put words in, and I have to obey) they say for the wagons they are fighting for them to go on. But I fear the result of this battle. The Lord have mercy on you. Do not move."

I replied to this letter as follows:

"MRS. KELLY:

"If you are really a white woman captive in the hands of these Indians, I shall be glad to buy you and restore you to your friends, and if a few unarmed Indians will deliver you at the place where your letter was received, I will send there for them three good American horses, and take you to our camp.

"I can not allow any party of Indians, few or many, to come to my train, or camp, while in this country.

"Tell them I shall move when I get ready, and halt as long as I think proper. I want no advice or favor from the Indians who attacked, but am prepared to fight them as long as they choose to make war. I do not, in the least, fear the result of this battle.

"Hoping that you may be handed to us at once for the offer I have made,

"I am truly,

(Signed)   "Jas. L. Fisk, Capt. Comd'g."

The above letter was sent back by the Indian messenger, and we awaited the result. In the afternoon we received the following reply:

"I am truly a white woman, and now in sight of your camp, but they will not let me go. They say they will not fight, but don't trust them. They say, 'How d'ye do.' They say they want you to give them sugar, coffee, flour, gunpowder, but give them nothing till you can see me for yourself, but induce them, taking me first. They want four wagons, and they will stop fighting. They want forty cattle to eat; I have to write what they tell me. They want you to come here—you know better than that. His name Chatvanco and the other's name Porcupine. Read to yourself, some of them can talk English. They say this is their ground. They say, 'Go home and come back no more.' The Fort Laramie soldiers have been after me, but they (the Indians) run so; and they say they want knives and axes and arrow-iron to shoot buffalo. Tell them to wait and go to town, and they can get them. I would give them any thing for liberty. Induce them to show me before you give any thing. They are very anxious for you to move now. Do not, I implore you, for your life's sake.

"FANNY KELLY.

"My residence formerly Geneva, Allen County, Kansas."

I returned by the Indian the following reply:

"DEAR MADAM:

"Your second communication convinces me that you are what you profess to be, a captive white woman, and you may be assured that myself and my party are eager for release, but for the present I can not accede to the demands, or gratify the wants of your captors. We are sent on an important trust and mission, by order of the great War Chief at Washington, westward to the mountain region, with a small party of well-armed and determined men, feeling entirely capable of defending ourselves; but we are not a war party, and our train is not intended for war purposes. Powder and shot we have, but no presents for the hostile Indians.

"I am an officer of the Government, but am not authorized, by my instructions to give any thing but destruction to Indians who try to stop me on my march. However, I will, for your release, give three of my own horses, some flour, sugar, and coffee, or a load of supplies. Tell the Indians to go back for the night, and to-morrow at noon, if they will send you with five men to deliver you to my soldiers on the mound we occupied to-day, their main body not to advance beyond their present position, I will hand over to them the horses and provisions, which they will be permitted to take away to their headquarters.

"Should there be occasion, the same opportunity for communicating will be granted to-morrow.

"The Great Spirit tells me that you will yet be safely returned to your friends, and that all wrongs that have been committed on the defenseless and innocent shall be avenged.

"In warmest sympathy, I am, Madam,

"JAS. L. FISK,
"Capt. and A. Q. M. U. S. A."

*   *   *   *   *   *   *

With high regard, I have the honor to be,
        Yours, very truly,

JAS. L. FISK,
Capt. and A. Q. M. Commanding Expedition.

ADJUTANT GENERAL'S OFFICE,
    WASHINGTON, March 17, 1870.
      OFFICIAL EXTRACT.

WM. BEECH,
Assistant Adjutant General.

STATEMENT OF LIEUTENANT G. A. HES-SELBERGER.

WASHINGTON, D. C., Feb'y 16, 1870.

To the Hon. JAMES HARLAN,

Chairman Com. Ind. Affairs, U. S. Senate.

SIR:

I have the honor to make the following statement in relation to the captivity and release of Mrs. Fanny Kelly.

In the summer of 1864, an expedition under the command of General Alfred Sully, U. S. A., started against the hostile Sioux in Dakota Territory, of which expedition I was a member, being then an officer, First Lieutenant, in the Sixth Iowa Volunteer Cavalry. Whilst on the expedition, we ascertained that Mrs. Fanny Kelly was a prisoner of the Indians that we were then engaged against. After the command returned to Fort Rice, in Dakota Territory, news was received from Captain Fisk, an officer of the Engineer Department, U. S. A., that he was surrounded, and his train corralled by the same Indians that we had been fighting. I, with others, saw Fisk, and was personally told by him that he had received notes and letters of warning from Mrs. Kelly, telling him that he must not break his train, that the Indians intended to fall upon the two portions, if he did, and to massacre his guard and the emigrants and children with him.

In the fall, after the expedition had been abandoned, the troops were scattered at different posts along the Missouri River, I, with my company, being left at Fort Sully, Dakota Territory. About the latter part of November, an Indian came inside the post. I, being officer of the day, asked him what he wanted. He said he came a long way, and wanted to know if I was the "big chief," if so, he had a paper for me to see. He gave it to me. It was a sheet torn out of a business book, and numbered 76 in the corner. The substance of the letter was as follows:

"I write this letter, and send it by this Indian, but don't know whether you will get it, as they are very treacherous. They have lied to me so often; they have promised to bring me to town nearly every day. I wish you could do something to get me away from them. If they do bring me to town, be guarded, as they are making all kinds of threats and preparations for an attack. I have made a pencil of a bullet, so it might be hard to read. Please treat this Indian well. If you don't, they might kill me." After having the Indian remain for a few days, and giving him plenty to eat, he was sent on his return with a letter to Mrs. Kelly. A short time after this, one morning, we discovered, back of the Fort on the hill, a large body of Indians. The commanding officer was notified of the fact. He immediately gave orders to prepare the fort for defense. Since the warning received from Mrs. Kelly, we had been unusually watchful of the Indians. The fort was poorly constructed, having been built by soldiers for winter quarters. The Indians were notified not to approach the fort, and only the chiefs, who numbered ten or twelve, were allowed to come inside the gates, bringing with them Mrs. Kelly, and when inside the fort, the gates were immediately closed, shutting out the body of the Indians, who numbered about 1,000 to 1,200. A bargain was made for her, and the articles agreed upon were delivered for her in exchange.

I believe, and it was the opinion of others, that the advice and warning of Mrs. Kelly was very valuable to us, and was instrumental in putting us on our guard, and enabled us to ward off the threatened attack of the Indians. In my opinion, had the Indians attacked the fort, they could have captured it.

The day that Mrs. Kelly was brought into the fort was one of the coldest I ever experienced, and she was very poorly clad, having scarcely any thing to protect her person. Her limbs, hands, and face were terribly frozen, and she was put in the hospital at Fort Sully, where she remained for a long time, nearly two months, for treatment.

(Signed)   G. A. HESSELBERGER,
First Lieutenant U. S. Army.
Res. Leavenworth City.

———

TREASURY DEPARTMENT,
Second Auditor's Office, June 3, 1870.

The foregoing is a correct copy of the statement of Lieutenant Hesselberger on file in this office.

E. B. FRENCH.

STATEMENT OF OFFICERS AND MEMBERS OF THE SIXTH IOWA CAVALRY.

We, the undersigned, late officers and members of the Sixth Iowa Cavalry, being duly sworn, do hereby depose and say that, during the winter of the years 1864 and 1865, the said Sixth Iowa Cavalry was stationed, and doing military duty, at Fort Sully, in the Territory of Dakota; that we, in our respective military capacities, were present during the winter stated at the aforesaid post of Fort Sully. Deponents further say that, on or about the 6th day of December, in the year 1864, an Indian appeared before the fort, and signified to the officer of the day, Lieutenant G. A. Hesselberger, that he had something to communicate to those within the fort; and the said Indian was allowed to enter, and presented to the commanding officer, Major A. E. House, of the regiment before stated, a note, or letter, which letter we all thoroughly knew the purport of, and it was seen and read by————. It was written, or purported to be, by one Mrs. Fanny Kelly, who represented herself as a captive in the hands of certain Blackfeet Sioux Indians; and that, under a pretext of delivering her up to her people, they intended attacking the town or village to which they purposed going.

Deponents further say that, at the time of the receipt of this letter, the said Fort Sully was not in such a state of defense as would have enabled the garrison to hold it against the attack of any considerable body of men; that, in consequence of the receipt of said letter, Major House brought the cannon in position to bear on all sides of the fort, and otherwise ordered and disposed of the garrison to withstand any attempt to capture or destroy the fort.

Deponents further say that, on or about the 9th day of December, the said Mrs. Fanny Kelly was brought in as a captive and delivered by the Indians to the commanding officer at Fort Sully; that the Indians came up to the fort painted in war paint, and singing their war songs; that as soon as Mrs. Kelly was within the gates of the fort, they were closed, and all the Indians save those who had her directly in charge were shut out from entrance into said fort.

Deponents further say, that they verily believe, from information then gained, and from that which they afterward learned, it was the intention of the Indians to attack the fort, and they were only prevented from doing so by the preparations which the letter of warning from the said Mrs. Fanny Kelly had induced the commanding officer to make; and they verily believe that, had the attack been made without such preparations, it would have resulted in the capture of the fort and the massacre of its inmates; and such was the expressed opinion of nearly all the members of the said Sixth Iowa Cavalry then stationed therein; and further deponents say not.

Signed. {
JOHN LOGAN, *Capt. Co. K, Sixth Reg. Iowa Cavalry.*
DEAN CHEADLE, *O. S.* " " " "
JOHN M. WILLIAMS, *Q. M. S.* " " "
JOHN MAGEE, *Serg't Co.* H, " " "
JOHN COOPER, *Corp. Co. K,* " " "
MERIT M. OAKLEY, *Corp. Co. H,* " " "
}

Personally appeared before me, A. J. McKean, Clerk of the District Court, Linn County, State of Iowa, and made solemn oath that the foregoing is true and correct in all particulars, and that neither of the parties hereto subscribing is interested in any way in any effort which the said Mrs. Kelly may make, or has made, for indemnity, on this 22d day of January, A. D., 1870.

[SEAL.]

A. J. McKEAN,
Clerk District Court, Linn County, Iowa.

TREASURY DEPARTMENT, }
SECOND AUDITOR'S OFFICE, *December* 2d, 1870. }

I certify the foregoing to be a true copy of the original filed in this office.

E. B. FRENCH,
Second Auditor.

[*The memoranda below are written with pencil.*]

Captain Logan was the officer of the day when Mrs. Kelly was brought into the fort (Sully).

John Magee, Sergeant Co. H. Sixth Iowa Cavalry, was sergeant of the guard at the same time.

To HON. JAMES HARLAN, U. S. S., and HON. WM. SMYTH, M. C., Second Congressional District, Iowa:

GENTLEMEN:—

I was at Fort Sully when the arrangement was made for the capture of this woman. Was not there when the Indians brought her into the fort; but am satisfied that the above affidavit, in the main, is correct.

(Signed.)

T. S. BARDWELL,
Late Assistant Surgeon Sixth Iowa Cavalry.

TREASURY DEPARTMENT,
SECOND AUDITOR'S OFFICE, *December* 24, 1870. }

I certify the foregoing to be a true copy of the original filed in this office.

E. B. FRENCH,
Second Auditor.

Printed in the United States
54594LVS00001B/26